"In a world of broken promises Rick Stedman lead[...]
Substantive yet simple, this super-practical guide is [...]
be transformed by the power of Jesus' promises. In yo[...]
easy to remember but profound in its depth. I want e[...]

Ben Cachiaras
Senior pastor, Mountain Christian Church, Baltimore, MD

"*Praying the Promises of Jesus* is exceptional because it pinpoints the essence of our trust-based relationship with Jesus. That trust is anchored in the promises that Jesus has made to each of us, which are inviolable and everlasting. In addition to his illuminating writing, Dr. Stedman's book furnishes us with actionable prayers that equip us with new tools to deepen a trust-based relationship with our God."

Steven C. Currall, Ph.D.
Professor of Management
Former dean of the Business School of Management
University of California, Davis

"In a world filled with broken promises and little hope, *Praying the Promises of Jesus* encourages us that Jesus' promises are real, they will not be broken, and they are for us today. Rick lays out a path to use the Scriptures as a part of our prayer vocabulary. What better way to communicate with God than by using His own Word? I highly recommend this book to anyone who wants to have an effective and powerful prayer life."

Chad Hennings
Founder, Wingmen Ministries
Dallas Cowboys three-time Super Bowl champion
US Air Force fighter pilot

"If you're looking for a field map to help you find the peace and power of Christ in your life, this is it."

Brian Jones
Author of *Second Guessing God*
Senior pastor, Christ's Church of the Valley, Royersford, PA

"With a graceful and inspirational voice, Pastor Rick teaches us how to access the inherent power in the promises of Jesus through daily audible prayer. *Praying the Promises of Jesus* is heavenly affirmation that God's promises are always true and they hold infinite power to transform our lives."

Kenneth B. Morris, Jr.
President, Frederick Douglass Family Initiatives
Great-great-great grandson of Frederick Douglass
Great-great grandson of Booker T. Washington

"You would think, after so many years in ministry, I would have some advice to offer on the subject of prayer. I don't. In this arena, I'm still a novice, seeking rather than dispensing counsel.

"I found in Rick Stedman a helpful guide. The longtime pastor has devoted himself to the study of scriptures related to prayer. On these pages he generously shares what he has learned. In *Praying the Promises of Jesus*, you will be impressed with Rick's personal practice of prayer and his desire to help others discover the same joy he has found in his disciplined walk with his promise-giving, promise-keeping Lord."

> **LeRoy Lawson, Ph.D.**
> Distinguished Professor of Christian Ministries
> Director of Doctor of Ministry Program
> Emmanuel Christian Seminary at Milligan College

"This is a wonderful book. It is insightful, practical, and deeply biblical. Rick Stedman understands that prayer is about bringing our hearts into alignment with God's heart, and he here presents an appealing and encouraging paradigm for making the practice of prayer a part of daily life. This book will reward the reader, serving as an encouragement to live in the presence and the will of God."

> **David Nystrom**
> Author, NIV Application Commentary, *James*
> Former Provost and Senior Vice President, Biola University

"A promise is an express assurance on which expectations are to be based. Rick's admonition on prayer is powerful and vital for believers to experience transformation of both life outlook and experience."

> **John E. Wasem**
> US Mobilization Director, Stadia

"In our effort to walk beside victims of sex trafficking on their journey of healing, I have found nothing more dependable than the promises of Jesus. I hang on to them for myself and our girls. I would recommend this book to anyone on any journey."

> **Jenny Williamson**
> Founder/CEO Courage Worldwide,
> working to eradicate sex trafficking worldwide

PRAYING THE PROMISES OF JESUS

RICK STEDMAN

HARVEST HOUSE PUBLISHERS
EUGENE, OREGON

Cover by Garborg Design Works

Backcover author photo by Jodi Burgess

Published in association with Books & Such Management, 52 Mission Circle, Suite 122, PMB 170, Santa Rosa, CA 95409-5370, www.booksandsuch.com.

PRAYING THE PROMISES OF JESUS

To Dean and Marcia Holst:
In-laws by marriage,
friends by choice,
and exemplary promise-makers and promise-keepers.

Contents

PART ONE

Why Pray the Promises of Jesus?

1

The Greatest Promise-
Maker of All Time

"The future is as bright as the promises of God."
ADONIRAM JUDSON

What if every promise of Jesus came true in your life?

Jesus was the ultimate promise-maker and promise-keeper, and among the many astonishing promises to his followers were these: to love us, to fill us with joy, to strengthen us, to give us peace and rest, and to prepare an eternal home for us.

Would you like your life to be molded and shaped by these promises of Jesus rather than by the broken promises of this world? Would you like to see Jesus' promises come true for those you love? Our lives—and the lives of our loved ones—can be transformed as we learn to pray the promises of Jesus daily.

If you want your life to change, the power is in the promises.

I invite you to journey with me in the pages of this book as we learn to pray the promises of Jesus. The promises of Jesus are incredibly powerful, and praying his promises is an effective and enjoyable way to pray. After all, we have the perfect model for both prayer and promises—Jesus himself.

Jesus—A Prolific Promise-Maker

Jesus was the greatest promise-maker and promise-keeper who ever lived. He made promises to his disciples, the crowds, and his opponents. He promised grieving sisters, a humble centurion, a penitent thief on an adjacent cross, and even those who called for his execution. Almost everywhere he went and to whomever he spoke, he made quite remarkable promises:

- "Heaven and earth will pass away, but my words will never pass away" (Luke 21:33).
- "Don't be afraid; just believe, and she will be healed" (Luke 8:50).
- "You will see heaven open" (John 1:51).
- "Anyone who eats my flesh and drinks my blood has eternal life, and I will raise that person at the last day" (John 6:54 NLT).
- "In My Father's house are many dwelling places; if it were not so, I would have told you; for I go to prepare a place for you" (John 14:2 NASB).
- "And you will see the Son of Man sitting at the right hand of the Mighty One and coming on the clouds of heaven" (Mark 14:62).
- "All authority in heaven and on earth has been given to me...And surely I am with you always, to the very end of the age" (Matthew 28:18,20).
- "Look, I am coming soon!" (Revelation 22:7).

Jesus was not shy about making promises. Students of the Bible have compiled different lists of the promises of Jesus, some of which number in the hundreds. As these lists show, Jesus was a prodigious promise-maker.

Plus, Jesus was a promise-keeper. When he said he would do something, he did it—no matter how impossible sounding or far-fetched.

Jesus used promises to shape the future of his followers' lives. Through making and keeping promises, Jesus reached into their tomorrows and changed the course and content of their lives. The promises of Jesus were exceedingly powerful:

- To several unknown fishermen, Jesus said, "Come, follow me, and I will send you out to fish for people" (Mark 1:17). As a result, these few men changed the world.

- To a grief-stricken father whose daughter had died, Jesus said, "Don't be afraid; just believe, and she will be healed" (Luke 8:50). To everyone's astonishment, Jesus kept that promise.

- He asked two of his followers to walk into a city where they would find a colt, and he promised that the owner would allow them to borrow it. When this came to pass, the followers learned that Jesus' promises even had power over future events (Matthew 21:1-6).

- To his confused disciples, Jesus said he would be tortured, killed, and then "on the third day he [would] rise again" (Luke 18:33). What type of man makes promises about dying and coming back to life and keeps them—on schedule? Yet Jesus did just that.

- Jesus told his disciples, "You will all fall away...but after I have risen, I will go ahead of you into Galilee." An overconfident Peter promised, "Even if all fall away, I will not." Jesus responded, "Truly I tell you...before the rooster crows twice you yourself will disown me three times" (Mark 14:27-30). Peter broke his promise whereas Jesus kept his, which is a foreshadowing of how we may break our promises to the Lord, but he never will.

- Before his ascension, Jesus told his followers to remain in Jerusalem and wait for the gift the Father had promised; they waited and were filled with the Spirit on the Day of Pentecost (Acts 1:4-8; 2:1-4). They changed from confused followers to confident witnesses.

Through this process of promise-making and promise-keeping, Jesus influenced his followers. He transformed them into better people than they were before. He took the unfinished clay of their lives and, through the power of promises, molded—and fired!—them into remarkable world-changers. He took weak, impulsive, fearful, doubtful people and, through the miracle of commitments, forged them into a confident force that altered history.

Would you like the promises of Jesus to come true in your life? To have your life molded and shaped by his promises rather than by the broken promises of this world? To experience the power of Jesus' promises today? If so, let's pray together this prayer:

Lord,

> You did an amazing thing in the lives of the apostles.
> You took average, diverse, and unimpressive men and transformed them into some of the most influential people the world has ever known. Fearful, impulsive, and faithless men became towering figures of faith, peace, and courage. Angry, unhappy, and lonely individuals discovered love, friendships, and community.
> Incredibly, you did this not while you were with them, but after you were crucified, buried, and risen. You were able to strongly affect them, even after your death, through the power of your promises, enabled by the Holy Spirit.
> Based on that evidence, I ask you to do the same in my life. Transform my doubts into faith and my fear into courage; change my worries to peace and my anxieties to rest; turn my sadness to joy and my loneliness to love. May I learn to live according to your promises, through the power of your Spirit.
> In your name I pray. Amen.

Practical Prayer Pointers

If you are like most readers, I'll bet that you read that prayer silently rather than audibly. If that is the case, I beg you to give this a try: pray the prayers in this book aloud, even though it might seem unnecessary or uncomfortable at first. There are many advantages and biblical reasons for praying out loud, which I will discuss in some of the sidebars in this book. The first biblical reason is this: 99.9 percent of all prayers in the Bible are vocalized. In fact, one has to work very hard to find even a few clear examples of silent, inaudible prayer. And even these may, at closer look, not refer to truly silent prayers.[1]

I believe that audible praying is an excellent way to grow in one's prayer ability. Of course, there is nothing wrong with praying silently in one's mind rather than vocally through one's mouth. The Bible is clear that God can read our thoughts (Genesis 6:5; 1 Chronicles 28:9; Psalm 139:2-4; Jeremiah 12:3), so he hears our silent prayers just as he does our vocalized prayers.

Silent prayer is not a sin—but it may surprise you to learn that it is not as biblical as praying aloud. In addition, I also suggest, in subsequent sidebars, that silent prayers are not as effective either. Could it be that current levels of prayerlessness and dissatisfaction with prayer among evangelical Christians might partially be due to a simple lack of praying aloud?

In my experience as a pastor, almost all Christians pray silently in their private prayer times and miss out on the many benefits of oral prayer. So if you speak to God from your heart but not with your lips in the majority of your prayers, why not try the other manner of praying that is vastly more common in Scripture?

Praying the Promises of Jesus Daily

As we have seen, Jesus was a fabulous promise-maker and promise-keeper. But can his promises come true in our lives? How do we access the power of Jesus' promises and actually experience their fulfillment today? The answer is the premise of this book: the promises of Jesus become realized in our lives through prayer. Our lives—and the lives of those we love—are transformed for the better as we learn to pray the promises of Jesus daily.

Since this book is about prayer, let's pause and talk to God about this rather than just think about it. Take a few seconds and pray this prayer aloud:

> Dear Lord,
>
> > Could this be true? Could my life be dramatically changed
> > for the better by the promises you have made?
> > If so, I ask you to shape my life, my plans, my relationships,
> > and my destiny through your promises. I pray that
> > your promises, Jesus, would gain control of my beliefs,
> > thoughts, and behaviors. May my life become what you
> > always have intended it to be.
> > In your name I pray. Amen.

A Map for Our Journey

In this book, we will travel together the path of prayer, discovering how to pray more effectively and enjoyably by praying the promises of Jesus. I've divided our journey into three different legs. In part 1, we will discover why the promises of Jesus are powerful, and how he uses them to shape and mold our lives. Along the way, we will also grasp why promises are essential in relationships and why broken promises are so damaging. Here we will reaffirm the need to be better promise-makers and promise-keepers ourselves.

In part 2, we will learn how to pray the promises of Jesus based upon a method I stumbled upon several years ago. At that time, I was concerned about the reality of spiritual warfare, and decided to do what I could to better protect my family members and friends from the attacks of the evil one. So I began to pray the armor of God for those I love, one piece per day of the week. As I described in the first book in this prayer series, *Praying the Armor of God*, I found that to be an easy, enjoyable, and effective way to pray.

In time, I began to associate other biblical lists with the days of the week. I began to pray the fruit of the Spirit, the Beatitudes, the Lord's Prayer, and the Psalms. And, of course, I began to systematically pray the promises of Jesus.

I chose the promises of Jesus because of the inherent power in his promises, and their potential to transform not only the present, but also the *futures* of those for whom I prayed. I arranged the promises into seven general categories, and then assigned each category to a day of the week. In this way, I was able to easily memorize and pray key promises of Jesus:

> **S**unday: I'm **S**urrounded by love.
>
> **M**onday: I'm **M**aking happiness a habit.
>
> **T**uesday: I'm **T**rusting in Gods' strength.
>
> **W**ednesday: I'm **W**anting what God wants.
>
> **Th**ursday: I'm **T**rading my troubles for peace.
>
> **F**riday: I'm **F**inding freedom.
>
> **S**aturday: I'm **S**o excited about heaven.

Once we memorize these days and categories, we can keep Jesus' promises in our minds all day long. If our thoughts wander away from God, it is easy to remember the day's promise. For instance, we might think, *Well, since it is Wednesday, the promises of today start with a W. Oh yeah—I'm Wanting what God wants.* In this prayer method, Wednesdays are dedicated to praying the promises of Jesus about God's will. On the midpoint of the week, we focus on what God wants, and we ask for our hearts to be changed so that we grow to desire what God desires. We remember how Jesus prayed about God's will in the Garden of Gethsemane, "Father, if you are willing, take this cup from me; yet not my will, but yours be done" (Luke 22:42). And we recall that he promised, "Very truly I tell you, my Father will give you whatever you ask in my name" (John 16:23). Based on these great and precious promises, we ask for God's will to be done in our lives, into the lives of those we love, and into the lives of anyone else that crosses our paths that day.

On some days I pray in this manner only once or twice, but on other days this becomes a theme that I return to over and over, and I find myself praying without ceasing. On *Sundays* I walk by people in church and pray for them to feel *Surrounded by love.* I drive through our city on

Mondays and ask God to *Make happiness a habit* in the homes that I pass. I watch the evening news on *Thursdays* and find myself praying that the people in the news stories would *Trade their troubles for peace*, because the peace of Jesus is the best solution to the problems in our world today. On *Fridays* I may walk through our neighborhood and pray for each family to discover the *Freedom* of God in Christ. I find myself obeying Paul's directive to "pray continually" (1 Thessalonians 5:17) as my heart seems to beat to the rhythm of each promise on its assigned day.

In part 3, we will practice praying the promises of Jesus daily through the use of guided prayers. I recommend that you commit to a four-week prayer adventure, which will take less than five minutes a day each morning and can then fill your mind and soul for the rest of the day.

Each week illustrates different ways to pray the promises of Jesus and utilizes numerous Scriptures as the content of the prayers. In the beginning, I recommend that you pray these prayers aloud, verbatim. Over time, you will gradually acclimate to this method of praying Scripture, and you will find yourself automatically memorizing many words and phrases. Feel free to adapt these prayers to your own style and manner, since getting rigid or legalistic about prayer is counterproductive. The goal is personalization rather than rote memorization. Gradually you will find that your prayer confidence and vocabulary increase, and you will hear yourself praying many of these scriptural phrases in different contexts, such as a table grace, a small group prayer time, or even while leading a congregational prayer in church.

After a small section that teaches what I call Daily Prayer Openers, the four weeks are divided in this way:

- Week One: Starting to Pray the Promises of Jesus

- Week Two: Praying the Promises of Jesus for Others

- Week Three: Praying the Promises of Jesus as Reflected in the Old Testament

- Week Four: Praying the Promises of Jesus as Reflected in the New Testament

After the four weeks, you may choose to repeat the cycle again, and again, and again. Or you may choose to focus on certain weeks that are closer to your heart. Feel free to park on a particularly meaningful week and pray it several weeks in a row until you feel released to move on. Also, feel free to skip a week if it is not helpful for you.

Before we launch into learning about the power of the promises of Jesus, let's pray:

Dear Jesus,

I marvel when I consider your closeness to the Father, the intimate relationship you had with him every day. On many days you met him early in the morning to talk, on others you spoke with him as the need arose, and occasionally you spent the whole night in prayer. You felt so close to him that you called him "Abba," and you were certain that he always heard your requests.

Yet you seemed to have a freedom and flexibility in your prayer life, and never became ensnared in legalistic traps. Your prayers were based not on rigid formulas but on a real relationship with the Father and Spirit.

So help me, as I go through the suggested prayers in this book, to remember that it's all about learning to talk naturally with you and developing a life with you always on my mind and in my heart.

In your precious and patient name I pray. Amen.

Practical Prayer Pointers

In the do-your-own-thing era of the seventies, we teenagers were suspicious of anything that appeared canned or false. Free-form was in vogue in everything from modern art to poetry. In the church, this meant that we were suspicious of prewritten prayers, which seemed to lack spontaneity and authenticity. So we opted for free-form prayers.

Honestly, most of them were awful. The same phrases repeated over and over, much more often than we would ever do in normal conversation: *Lord I just want to ask...I just want to say...I just-just-just.* Or they sounded like this: *God I really...really...really.* Or *Father-God...Father-God...Father-God,* as if it were one word rather than two. Plus, the prayers lacked variety and depth. Just the same-old same-old, again and again.

Then I was taught to pray Scripture—aloud. Immediately, I felt like my prayer life jumped from kindergarten into college. And even though I didn't write them out, my public prayers took on a new depth and breadth. I began to hear myself praying in public what I had prayed aloud in private, the words of Scripture, adapted as appropriate: "Lord, I pray that the eyes of their hearts be enlightened, that they may know the hope to which you have called us...I ask that their love may abound more and more in knowledge and depth of insight...I pray that you would help them not concern themselves with great matters or things too wonderful for them...I ask that goodness and mercy will follow them all the days of their lives, and that they will dwell in the house of the Lord forever..." (Ephesians 1:18, Philippians 1:9, Psalm 131:1; 23:6).

As a result, I wholeheartedly encourage you, in your private times of prayer, to pray aloud. Pray with your Bible open, and as you read a passage and think of a person to whom it may apply, pray it for him or her. Pray the Psalms, the Proverbs, and the whole New Testament. Pray the prayers in this book, aloud, and over and over. Authenticity and repetition are not mutually exclusive.

2

The Power of Promises

"When we make promises, we reach into tomorrow's
oceans of uncertainty and create islands of security."
LEWIS SMEDES

G od is the ultimate promise-maker and promise-keeper. The Bible is chock-full of the promises of God, and Jesus, in the Gospels, stays true to form. The promises of Jesus hold vast power to shape our lives. His promises have the power to provide for us, his followers, the lives we have been longing for.

If you want your life to change, the power is in the promises. It is through promises that God transforms our lives, which is why both making and keeping promises are so important. But before I explain why promises are so powerful, allow me to address the skeptics among us.

"But He Broke His Promise…"

Some of you may be very skeptical—even suspicious—about promises. If so, I don't blame you. After all, our lives are littered with the painful debris of broken promises.

"She promised to be faithful."

"He promised we would get married."

"My parents promised they would never get divorced."

"But my boss promised me a raise."

"My business partner promised to be honest this time."

"I voted for him because he promised so many things."

So many broken promises clutter the landscape of our lives that it makes me wonder: why do we still make promises—tons of them—in spite of the dismal track record of our species?

I think it's because we humans are, at our core, promise-making beings. Even people who give up on promises and assert they will never make any more—well, that's a promise to themselves. This suggests that we are hard-wired to make promises; we can't avoid them.

This is a shocking truth, especially when we consider that so many of the promises made today are not kept. Millions of couples marry each year, in spite of the huge number of divorces. Business people sign contracts, but only after inserting enough legal loopholes so they can back out if needed. We make New Year's resolutions, which are promises to ourselves, even though studies show we often abandon them in less than a week. Politicians may take the cake in this area: they make promises and then break them so routinely that it almost seems part of the job description.

We are promise-making beings, but also profoundly bad at keeping those promises. We go steady, shake hands, sign contracts, and cross-our-hearts-hope-to-die. Then we break up, shake our fists at one another, nullify agreements, and accuse one another of cheating hearts.

If you want proof that we humans are poor promise-keepers, just listen to country western music for a while. I'll bet that you hear two recurring themes: people believe in God, and they cheat on their spouses. How messed up is that?

Carrie Underwood sang both "Jesus Take the Wheel" (2005) and "Before He Cheats" (2006). Hank Williams's top hits include "Your Cheatin' Heart" (1953) and "I Saw the Light" (1948). Sometimes the songs are autobiographical. Randy Travis put out several gospel albums, but only after justifying his own marital failures in "Reasons I Cheat" (1986). Alan Jackson's *Precious Memories II* was named Top Christian Album at the 2014 Billboard Music Awards, and he also admitted to infidelity when his recording of "Who's Cheatin' Who?" (1997) was at the top of the charts. Shania Twain sang, "Whose Bed Have Your Boots Been Under?" (1995), and then divorced her husband when she discovered the bed was her best friend's. Some songs even get violent: in

Miranda Lambert's "Kerosene" (2005), the jilted spouse leaves a smoldering corpse behind, literally.

Why this detour into musical celebrities and hits? The point is this: songs don't become popular unless they hit a deep emotional chord with the listeners. And songs about infidelity and broken promises do just that: they express what so many people feel, which is hurt and betrayal due to broken promises. This hurt is common to us all, which is why the songs first hit a nerve, and then hit the top of the charts.

If you have been hurt by broken promises, then I encourage you to join me in this prayer:

Dear Lord,

> There are so many things I desire in life, so many dreams I have deep in my heart. I desire to love and be loved, to have a healthy and loving family, and to have a marriage that lasts a lifetime (if single: friendships that last a lifetime).
> But I know these things require commitments, and because I've been deeply wounded by broken promises, I'm afraid to trust promises anymore—even my own. So help me, dear Lord, to overcome my fears and learn anew the value of promises.
> In humble hope, I pray. Amen.

Practical Prayer Pointers

Learning to pray is like learning new vocabulary words or even an entire language. To learn new words, it is best to speak them vocally, not silently. As we say words aloud, we mold them in our mouths, infuse them with our breath, and feel them with our teeth and tongues; we almost taste their form and structure. If we do this often enough, our body will form the habit of saying the word. Muscle memory and synaptic patterns help us remember the word later, even entire phrases and prayers. For instance, many people can repeat the Lord's Prayer or the Apostles' Creed, though they have never tried to memorize either. They just repeated the words, aloud, week after week in their childhood church. In time, they not only knew the prayers, but also could pray them aloud in public.

In like fashion, I recommend that the prayers in this book be prayed aloud. Even a whisper is better than silence. And don't be afraid of praying the same prayers over and over. In time, this will increase your personal prayer vocabulary, as well as your felicity in prayer. In time, it will be easier for you to pray audibly with others, whether one-on-one, in small groups, or even in large settings. You will be able to say publicly what you have said many times in private.

Why Do We Keep Making Promises?

If humans are so shockingly poor at keeping promises and broken promises are so painful, then the logical question is: why do we keep making them? Don't you think, if secular evolutionists are correct, that this behavior would have been extinguished long ago? Are we masochists or just foolish?

I think the answer is neither. Instead, maybe we are inveterate promise-makers because God is a promise-maker, and we are created in his image (Genesis 1:26-27). Throughout the Bible, God makes promises. To Adam and Eve, both before and after the fall, and even to their son, Cain. To Noah and his family. To Abraham, Isaac, and Jacob. The list is endless. The God revealed in the Bible is a persistent promise-maker.

Plus, God is the consummate promise-keeper. God, unlike humans, keeps his promises. Every one. 100 percent. No exceptions. God is the ultimate promise-maker and promise-keeper (Psalm 145:13). But why does God make promises? Why does he not just act in the present, rather than make promises about the future?

The answer to this question has at least two parts, so here's the first part: *Promises are God's tool to fix what's broken in this universe—especially us.*

I'm convinced that promises are one way God fine-tunes our lives, to help us achieve lives brimming with love, happiness, and fulfillment. His promises have the power to improve our lives tremendously and enable us to become all that God created us to be. A promise is an incredible, powerful tool.

I've always loved tools. During college I worked at a welding supply company, and we all had nicknames based on our favorite tools. One guy was Torch, because his solution to every problem was, "Let me burn it off." Another employee was Duct Tape, another the Hammer, and I was Vise Grips (still my favorite tool to this day).

A promise is also a tool, but an absolutely unique one. Most tools shape existing objects: a saw shapes a piece of wood, and a file molds a piece of metal. But a promise is extraordinary because it doesn't shape a tangible item. Instead, a promise shapes *the future*.

Think about tomorrow. What will happen? The potential events that could occur are innumerable, more than the grains of sand on a beach. Tomorrow is a blank canvas, a tabula rasa, an exponential mass of potentialities. It is formless and empty, like the heavens and earth in the opening verses of Genesis. It is a wild, complete unknown.

But into the vacuous emptiness of tomorrow, a promise reaches out and gives shape to the future. A promise—catch this!—creates the future. In the classic words of Lewis Smedes (depicted in the opening words of this chapter), "When we make promises, we reach into tomorrow's oceans of uncertainty and create islands of security."[1] Wow. In my opinion, that is one of the best phrases ever formulated.

How does this work? Well, let me give you an example. While writing the last paragraph, one of my sons texted me and asked if we could talk on the phone tomorrow. Due to the busyness of his college life, we decided to set a phone appointment for tomorrow evening at eight o'clock. Suddenly, the future begins to take shape. Together, he and I have reached out into the formless abyss of tomorrow's unknowns and have established a known point of contact. Into the chaos of tomorrow's randomness, we have brought a bit of order.

Actually, I have been doing this for him since his birth. Unbeknownst to him, when he was born I made an unvoiced promise. In my heart, I intentioned: *My boy, as long as God gives me breath, I will always be there for you. No matter what the future holds, you can count on me. I promise.*

In that act, I reached out into the years of tomorrows and brought structure into my life as well as his. He wasn't able to comprehend it at the time, and honestly neither was I. I was pledging myself to him unilaterally. *Son, as far as it is possible with me, in the future you always will find me there with you, present in spirit, if not physically.*

Till Death Do Us Part…

The promises I made to him (and his siblings) were based on earlier promises I made to his mother, Amy, my wife of over twenty-five years. Even before he was conceived, I promised his mother "to love and honor, for richer or poorer, for better or worse, in sickness and in health, till death do us part." Before that promise (and her reciprocal promise to me), Amy and I lived separate lives. I didn't even know she existed until about two years before that moment. Our lives could have diverged in a zillion different ways.

But on our marriage day, young and naïve as we were, we exchanged promises. We stretched out together, in hope and faith, and grasped the future. A few words brought contour to countless future moments. Today, though our roads may diverge due to work, errands, or whatever, I know that at the end of the day, she will come home. And I will do the same. Unless something tragic—God forbid—intervenes, we will be together tonight…and tomorrow night…and the night after…till death do us part. One simple, mutual promise created a different—and much better—future for us both.

Amy and I also have promised each other to never divorce. In fact, we have a "We Will Never Divorce" certificate taped to our bedroom mirror, signed and dated by us both. (A few years ago, hundreds of couples in our church did the same. It was our congregation's way of stemming the tide of marital failures in our little corner of the world.) Our children have seen this certificate, and they know how thoroughly we are committed to one another. This lifelong promise has created, for our kids, a home that is an island of security in a world of insecure relationships. No matter how confusing or chaotic a particular day might be, they know that when they come home, it will be to parents who are still together and to a family that will always be there for one another.

They have seen the parents of their close friends divorce, and they have witnessed the pain and lasting damage that resulted. But we have determined—we have promised—that they will never have to worry about that in our home. And they know that Amy and I are not perfect. We get mad at each other at times, act in immature ways (okay, that one is more my issue than hers), and even, on occasion, fight in front of our kids. The point: even imperfect people can keep difficult promises.

And the promises she and I made to each other were, in turn, made possible by the promise-making and promise-keeping parents that we both are blessed to have. Our parents made similar vows and kept them for a lifetime. As did our grandparents, great-grandparents, and on and on. Is it too much to say that my daily life is still shaped by the promises made in generations past? I think not. Our ability to keep our promises to each other is heavily influenced by our parents' and grandparents' faithfulness.

(This is one reason I chose to dedicate this book to my in-laws, Dean and Marcia Holst. Their example of faithfulness and promise-keeping in marriage contributed, I believe, to Amy's ability to do the same in our marriage. So if you are reading this, thanks again, Dean and Marcia.)

To sum it up: our lives are shaped by our promises, built on the promises of others, and again on those of still others. We are indeed promise-making beings.

Humans are known as *homo sapiens*, which in Latin means "wise man." But as I look at the current insanity of our world—the wars, unnecessary sufferings, addictions, and dysfunctions—I wonder if the designation "wise" fits our species. Maybe what defines us is not wisdom, but our ability to transcend time, to reach into our tomorrows and make and keep promises. Maybe we should be called *homo promittens*, which is the Latin word for "promising." Thus, *homo promittens* translates as "promising man," because *pro* means "forth" or "forward," and *mittere* means "to send." (Sorry, but *promittens* has nothing to do with gloves or mittens.) A promise is literally a "sending-forward," an act that reaches forward and changes tomorrow.

This is why, in spite of our bad track record, we can't help ourselves. We keep making promises. It's our nature. It's how we bring form to the future, how we turn dreams into reality. It's how hope becomes actual. When we make promises, we are like God: we create something that has never before existed. We are made in the image of God, and though we cannot create substances *ex nihilo*, we can bring appointments and future connections into existence. We can create tomorrow.

Dear Lord,

Thank you for the tremendous power you have given me
to reach out into tomorrow and create a better future
through making and keeping promises.
I want to be a person who is faithful and whose word is
true and trustworthy. I know your Word promises that
you will not forsake your faithful ones, so I want to be
that type of person.
So I ask, dear Jesus, please give me the strength to be like
you: a wise promise-maker and faithful promise-keeper.
In your grace. Amen.

Practical Prayer Pointers

How do silent prayers and audible prayers work together? It is my opinion that as we learn to pray better audibly, it increases our ability to pray better silently. However, the opposite is not always true. So I recommend, especially for new believers, a dedicated, private prayer time during the day in which you can learn the language and content of prayer. As you intone these prayers aloud, over and over, they become words and phrases that you can later call to mind. The audible words you have prayed will form linguistic habits and will become the go-to content of your silent prayers throughout the day.

Thus, vocalized prayers become the foundation upon which silent prayers can be built. Skyscrapers have deep concrete foundations, and the depth of the concrete footings determines the potential height of the building. In the same way, the depth of our audible, private prayers becomes the foundation for our silent, continual prayers.

Switching metaphors, we might say that prayer is similar to learning a foreign language in that expertise in speech precedes the ability to think in that language. In the same way, we learn to pray without ceasing after we have gained some expertise praying verbally, and especially praying Scripture aloud.

So promises are powerful tools that God uses to fix our brokenness and guide our futures. But how does God do this, and how does this relate to prayer? And on a more personal level, what can each of us do to make sure that God's promises come true in our lives? The answers to these questions await us in the next chapter.

3

How Promises Create Relationships

"A promise is the assurance that God gives to people so they can walk by faith while they wait for him to work."

JAMES MACDONALD[1]

The Bible is full of promises because, as we have seen, they are God's tools to fix what is broken. Since our world is broken in so many ways, God made a huge number of promises. God knew that the earth and its inhabitants would fall under the penalty of sin, resulting in brokenness and death. The cosmos would need to be fixed, and no repair was more important than our relationship with him. All of creation groans, frustrated by its bondage to death and decay (Romans 8:22). But only humans are self-conscious of that bondage, painfully aware that something is not right with this world and not right even in each person's inner world. We groan because we intuit that something is terribly wrong, and we groan because we are separated from God, the one in whom we were created to live and move and have our being (Acts 17:28).

How did God choose to fix such colossal brokenness? Of course, he could have just ordained the future plan of redemption and kept his intentions hidden from us. He might have chosen to take care of business by himself, as we do with our pets and houseplants. We arrange for their care but don't bother to inform them of the details. If God had done the same, that would have prevented us from having a part in the solution. For reconciliation to occur, both parties must be involved. So God's method to fix his broken creation was to use promises. In making promises, God *includes* us in the redemption story, and in the process heals not just all that is broken but also our personal, individual relationships with him.

This is why, throughout the Scriptures, God makes promises. For instance, God knew that he would choose a man, Abram, through whom all peoples on earth would be blessed (Genesis 12:1-3). God could have done just that without telling Abram or his descendants of his intentions. Instead, God promised himself to them in what was described as a covenant of love[2] (Deuteronomy 7:9). Slowly, God was doing two things. First, he was revealing his very nature to the people of earth: God is a God who makes and keeps promises. Second, God was, through promises, building trustworthy relationships with humans.

This became clear when God chose another man, Moses, to lead his people out of slavery. Again, God could have orchestrated events to unfold without ever telling Moses what he was doing; God could have executed the entire Exodus without explaining his plans. But God chose to reveal himself and his plans to Moses from within a burning bush, saying, "I have promised to bring you up out of your misery in Egypt...into a land flowing with milk and honey" (Exodus 3:17). God did not just make plans: he made promises. And in so doing, he built a relationship with Moses of fidelity, faithfulness, and—take a deep breath here—even friendship. After years of mutual promise-making and promise-keeping, the relationship between Moses and God grew to the point where "The LORD would speak to Moses face to face, as one speaks to a friend" (Exodus 33:11). This would have been impossible without the giving and keeping of promises.

Sadly, God also knew that his chosen people would break their side of the promises. He foreknew they would be unfaithful to him, would break the covenants, and would reap the natural consequences of their adultery. And though God foreknew their apostasy, he also prearranged their redemption. God planned, before the creation of the world (Revelation 13:8), to sacrifice his only begotten Son as the lamb who would purchase back, with his blood, humans for God (Revelation 5:9). God decided to fix everything and chose to let us in on his plans by revealing to us his promises. He revealed his plans to the prophets, who spoke of the consequences of sin and the promise of a messiah (Isaiah 9:1-7;

11:1-10; Daniel 7:13-14; Micah 5:1-5). He chose to make us heirs of promise (Ephesians 3:6) so that we could have a part in the unfolding drama of the ages.

How Friendships Are Forged

When we make and keep promises, we are like God. God is the one who started making promises, and we humans have been created in his image (Genesis 1:27). Only humans are like God in this capacity; neither animals nor angels, as far as we know, are equipped with this ability. And without this ability, relationships would be impossible. Neither friendships nor families could ever occur without promises. Promises are how relationships are created, shaped, and maintained.

Here we have arrived at the second answer to the question posed earlier: why does God use promises? The second part of my answer is: *Promises are how God creates relationships.*

It's the same for us. When two humans make and keep promises, they begin to build shared experiences and memories. "I'll see you at the pool tomorrow." "Let's walk home together after school." "Want to go on a date with me? Okay, I'll pick you up at seven." These types of promises, and millions more, shape our childhood and youthful friendships, and teach us both when to make promises and when not to: "I pledge allegiance to the flag," "I promise to take out the trash," "I will have my homework done by tomorrow," and "I promise to serve and defend my country." Over time, promises are vital ingredients in the maturation process, and also essential elements in relationship creation and preservation. We learn to be cautious in our promise-making, and dependable in our promise-keeping.

In time, youthful promises lead, for most young adults, to the big question: "Will you marry me?" If the beloved's response is yes, this adventure in promise-making and relationship-forging culminates in the most important promise two humans can exchange: wedding vows.

But even here, there is mass confusion in our culture. As a pastor, I have officiated at many weddings and, from time to time, a couple will request to write their own vows (this was especially true in the artsy 70s and 80s). In my early years of ministry, I would say, "Okay, but I get the right to edit or veto them." In short order I learned that most of them deserved the veto, a quick death, since they were vacuous and spineless. For instance, one couple wrote, "I promise to love you as long as our love shall last." I was shocked when I first heard those words. It was not a vow; it was a surrender-in-advance. How on earth would such a weak promise help the couple navigate the stormy and difficult seasons they would face? Another couple wrote, "I can't promise you forever, but I will promise you today." That was not a promise—it was literally a one-night stand.

The common element in these pseudo-vows was the underlying message: I promise to do such and such, *until I change my mind*. This is the polar opposite of the biblical term *faithfulness*, which is a character quality of God: "The one who called you is faithful, and he will do it" (1 Thessalonians 5:24). Moses, after years of walking with God, was able to declare, "Know therefore that the LORD your God is God; he is the faithful God, keeping his covenant of love to a thousand generations" (Deuteronomy 7:9). Faithfulness is also a virtue that is expected of Christ-followers: it is one of the types of the fruit of the Spirit (Galatians 5:23), and it is how we are to endure hard times—"patient in affliction, faithful in prayer" (Romans 12:12). Faithfulness means I will keep my promise to you, *and I won't change my mind*.

This brings to center stage a massive problem in our world today: choice now trumps promise. In fact, choice has been promoted from an ability to a *right*, and, as a result, rights seem to be multiplying like rabbits. In the past, rights were seen as God-given, and they existed because people had been "endowed by their Creator with certain inalienable rights." Today, rights are no longer delimited ("certain"), and any interest group can claim their perceived needs to be rights. What were once considered to be preferences or opportunities are now being elevated to the status of rights. It's a train that is out of control, which will lead not to more happiness but to more resentment.

Choice is in, and people today are prochoice in more areas than just reproduction. As a result, a promise no longer includes the notion that *I won't change my mind*. Even Christians have fallen under this spell: they cheat on their taxes and lie to their employers, though they sign documents that say they will be truthful. They take a sick day when, in fact, they just want a paid day off (is that stealing, lying, promise breaking, or all three?). As a pastor for over thirty years, I often was surprised at the trivial reasons Christians use to support switching churches, even though they had signed a membership covenant. And saddest of all, many Christians feel free to divorce their spouses regardless of the fact that they pledged "till death do us part."[3]

Since promise-making and promise-keeping are so important in marriages, I soon learned to steer couples away from writing their own vows. Instead, I encouraged them to stick with the tried and true, old-fashioned, traditional vows. Although there are slight differences depending upon one's denomination, here is the version I prefer:

> I take you to be my wedded wife (husband),
> to have and to hold from this day forward,
> for better or worse,
> for richer or poorer,
> in sickness and in health,
> to love, honor, and cherish,
> till death do us part.
> Before God and these people,
> I promise you my faithful love.

Those vows have teeth. They have substance. They close all loopholes. They negate the need for any prenuptial agreement. (What is a prenuptial anyway? Isn't it a doubt that the promise will be kept? An expectation of failure? A pre-nup is nothing but a give-up, signaled way in advance.)

Let's pray about this:

Dear Lord,
> I want to be a person who makes and keeps promises, but
>   it is so hard to make promises when the future seems
>   unsure. And it is even more difficult to keep promises
>   when storms arise and others break their promises to me.
> Help me to pattern my life not after my culture, where
>   promises are easily made and even more easily broken.

Teach me how to be more like you, Jesus, for all your
promises are true;
In fact, you are called "Faithful and True." Amen.

Practical Prayer Pointers

Learning to pray is like learning a new name. When meeting a person for the first time, experts suggest a great memory trick is to repeat the name immediately, and then use it *aloud* several times in your interaction with the person. "Nice to meet you, Rick. I have another friend named Rick, so your name is familiar to me already. Is Rick a family name, or were you named after someone specific?" I know this sounds wooden and stiff, but it is a great way to memorize names. In our church of several thousand people, I was able to recall tons of names due to this simple device. Try it—it works.

The same is true for prayer. Repeating the same phrase over and over—vocally—is a wonderful way to learn to pray.

Love Is…the Result of Promises Kept Over the Long Haul

What I am trying to say, in a world that devalues promise-making and -keeping, is that healthy promises are essential to healthy, relational living. Promises are the material from which friendships and families are forged; they are the fabric from which relationships can be sewn.

And as married couples who have been married for twenty, thirty, or forty years can attest, it is only after the feelings of infatuation diminish that the real bonds of love are formed. Love is patient and longsuffering, according to the apostle Paul (1 Corinthians 13:4-7); it takes time and endurance. In a word, faithfulness.

It is by making and keeping promises that true love is formed—that life together is built. We learn that trouble may come our way, but together we can survive almost any storm and overcome any obstacle. We gain confidence and become less fearful. We learn that joy shared is joy multiplied. Over time, the days of promise-making and promise-keeping add up to weeks and months, which in turn become years and decades. Lives built through faithfulness, whether expressed in deep friendship or in marriage, take on a depth and value that is hard to imagine in our days of youth.

How sad it is that many people today view commitments as limiting or restrictive. As one friend of mine said, "I didn't make promises when I was a young man because I thought I was keeping my options open." He later saw that the opposite was the case: his lack of commitments was hindering his friendships, stalling the development of family, and reducing the quality of his relationships. Later in life, he came to see that promises are what liberate us to build enduring futures and legacies, and unleash us to become more than we ever could have become on our own. The conclusion is clear: a person brings out the best in himself and in others by making and keeping meaningful promises.

This is why Jesus made promises to his disciples and followers-to-come. The promises of Jesus shape and form us into the persons we were created to be, thus developing in us the qualities of life that we all yearn for, such as love, peace, and hope. Through a relentless pursuit, the promises of Jesus transform not only us believers, but also are changing the quality of life on planet earth for the better. Faithfulness in his promises act much like a foundation of a home or building. Of course, we need good material in the right proportions and places, but it's all about the chief architect behind the project: God (Hebrews 11:10).

Before we move ahead to learn the daily method of praying the promises of Jesus, let's put together some of the prayers we have prayed thus far, and approach God in a summary prayer:

Dear Lord,

There are so many things I desire in life, dreams I have deep in my heart. I desire to love and be loved, to be in a loving family, and to have a marriage that lasts a lifetime (if single: friendships that last a lifetime).

But I know these things require commitments, and because I've been deeply wounded by broken promises, I'm afraid to trust promises anymore—even my own.

I want to be a person who is faithful, who makes and

keeps promises, and whose word is true and trustworthy. Your Word promises that you will not forsake your faithful ones.

But it is so hard to make promises when the future seems unsure. And it is even more difficult to keep promises when storms arise and others break their promises to me.

So I pray, dear Jesus, that you would give me the strength to be like you: a faithful promise-maker and promise-keeper. I pray that the promises you gave to your followers would come true in my life.

I long to be the person you created me to be, for you formed me in my mother's womb, and the plans you have for me are good.

In your name, which is Faithful and True. Amen.

PART TWO

An Easy Method to Pray
the Promises of Jesus

4

Sunday: I'm Surrounded by Love

"Life is full of misery, loneliness, and suffering.
And it's all over much too soon."

WOODY ALLEN

Years ago there was a game show called *Name that Tune* in which the contestants, music-lovers all, could often name a tune after hearing just three or four notes. Let's play a slightly altered version: given about three or four words from a song, can you fill in the missing word? Here we go:

- "Look at all the _____ people..."
- "One is the _____ number..."
- "I'm so _____ I could cry..."

The missing word in each case was "lonely" (or some version of it), which appears, often repeatedly, in scores[1] of rock and roll songs. One song by Sting takes the cake because he repeats "lonely" about sixty times. Sting named this song, naturally, "So Lonely."

Loneliness is a pervasive problem. It afflicts rich and poor, young and old, male and female, and even married and single. Mother Teresa said, "Loneliness and the feeling of being unwanted is the most terrible poverty."[2] Albert Schweitzer wrote, "We are all so much together, but we are dying of loneliness."[3] And author Tom Wolfe summed up the perspective of modern secularism, "The whole conviction of my life now rests upon the belief that loneliness, far from being a rare and curious phenomenon, peculiar to myself and to a few other solitary men, is the central and inevitable fact of human existence."[4]

Are you enjoying this talk about loneliness? Probably not. So let's change our tune. Since talking about loneliness is a bit of a downer, let's try another missing word game from songs:

- "_____ me tender..."
- "She _____ you, yeah, yeah, yeah..."
- "_____ makes the world go round..."

This answer is obvious: love. But (sigh and dramatic pause) love is so very, very hard to maintain. The Beatles said, "All you need is love" and then broke up. Toni Tennille sang, "Love will keep us together," and then divorced Captain. And after enduring years of abuse from her husband Ike, Tina Turner sang, "What's love got to do with it?"

So in rock and roll we have two of the great, universal themes of humanity: loneliness and love. Is that true in your life as well? Do you struggle with both loneliness and love? Do you wish there were a way to conquer loneliness and find lasting love? If so, I have great news for you: Jesus promises to help us achieve both.

Jesus' Promise of Love

Into this world filled with loneliness and failed love, Jesus made astonishing promises:

- "To all who received him, to those who believed in his name, he gave the right to become children of God" (John 1:12).
- "On that day you will realize that I am in my Father, and you are in me, and I am in you. Whoever has my commands and keeps them is the one who loves me. The one who loves me will be loved by my Father, and I too will love them and show myself to them" (John 14:20-21).

The solution to loneliness is lasting, enduring love. It is having at least one other person in your life who will never leave or abandon you, will never break his or her promises to you, and who will be an ongoing, reliable presence in your life. In essence, Jesus has promised to surround our lives with his love.

How can Jesus do this? How can he promise to immerse us in his never-ending love, and how can he be sure his promises will all come true?

The answer takes us deep inside the very nature of both God and love. The brilliant revelation from the Bible is this: God doesn't just love, but *is love*. For God, love is not merely a character quality, it is the essence of his being. This is why the Bible can say, "God is love" (1 John 4:8,16).

Though often oversimplified and misunderstood, this is the heart of the concept of the Trinity: God as three-in-one. Father, Son, and Holy Spirit. In the very core of God's being, love exists. God not only loves others, he loves within himself. God is a relational reality. Even before[5] the heavens and earth and all living things were created, God was giving and receiving love within "the Godhead" (Colossians 2:9 NKJV). In fact, the New Testament describes love as a quality of each of the three persons of the Trinity: "See what great love the Father has lavished on us" (1 John 3:1), "Having loved his own who were in the world, [Jesus] loved them to the end" (John 13:1), and "I urge you...by the love of the Spirit" (Romans 15:30).

God truly is love, which is why his love will never waver or end. Even he cannot change the essence of his own being, just as you and I cannot change the essence of our humanness. And since Jesus is God (John 20:28), he too cannot choose to be unloving. When Jesus promised to come to us and love us (John 14:21,23), he made a promise that is impossible for him to break.

Allow this to penetrate deep into your soul: the God of the entire universe loves you. His love was so great that he sacrificed his one and only Son for you (John 3:16). In love he has adopted you into his family (Ephesians 1:5), so you are secure in his loving arms. And for the rest of your life on earth—and for eternity in heaven (what an adventure!)— though you will grow in your understanding of God's love, you will never be able to grasp it entirely. It surpasses the capacities of human knowledge, because to know the fullness of God's love is to know the fullness of God himself, since God is love. This is why Paul wrote, "I pray that you, being rooted and established in love, may have power, together with all the Lord's holy people, to grasp how wide and long and high and deep is the love of Christ, and to know this love that surpasses knowledge—that you may be filled to the measure of all the fullness of God" (Ephesians 3:17b-19).

Let's talk with God about this.

> Dear Triune God, magnificent Three-in-One, the Godhead who does not merely love from time to time, but who is love, for love is your very being, and "God is love."
>
> How comforting it is to know that you have promised to adopt me into your family. Because I received Jesus as my Savior and Lord, you gave me the right to become one of your children, O God.
>
> Thank you for reaching out into my future and promising not only to adopt me, but to be in me and with me forever. Thank you for promising to come to me, in every moment of my life, and love me. Your love is better than any treasure and sweeter than the finest wine. Your love is new every morning—great is your faithfulness.
>
> In the name of the Father, Son, and Holy Spirit. Amen.

Jesus' Promise of Presence

In addition, Jesus promised to be perpetually present in our lives.

- "Where two or three gather in my name, there am I with them" (Matthew 18:20).
- "Surely I am with you always, to the very end of the age" (Matthew 28:20).

These last words in Matthew's Gospel (Matthew 28:20) record a mind-blowing promise. What could this possibly mean, other than a claim to divine omnipresence and ageless existence? The same is true of his promise to be in the midst of believers when two or more gather together (Matthew 18:20). Does this not imply a claim to be God? Yes on both counts: Jesus is God dwelling among us (John 1:14), and he is the promised Messiah who was given all authority, everlasting dominion, and is worthy of worship (Daniel 7:13-14; note the parallels to Matthew 28:18-20). Even one of the names given to Jesus, Immanuel, means "God with us" (Matthew 1:23).

God's presence in our lives is also a Trinitarian event. Jesus promised to be with us and also promised that the Spirit would be with us (John 16:7). But perhaps the most comforting promise is from God the Father, "Never will I leave you; never will I forsake you" (Hebrews 13:5).[6] It is often pointed out by Bible teachers that this verse is the strongest negative in the whole New Testament, comprised as it is of five negations: "I will no not leave you nor no not forsake you" (my translation). In English, this is poor grammar, but in Greek, it is a powerful way to convey the permanence of his promise.

Let this sink in as well: Jesus is always with you. Always. A prayer of the Irish church pioneer, known as Saint Patrick, expresses this well:

> Christ with me, Christ before me,
> Christ behind me, Christ in me,
> Christ beneath me, Christ above me,
> Christ on my right, Christ on my left,
> Christ when I lie down,
> Christ when I sit down,
> Christ when I arise,
> Christ in the heart of every man who thinks of me,
> Christ in the mouth of everyone who speaks of me,
> Christ in every eye that sees me,
> Christ in every ear that hears me.[7]

As a follower of Jesus, Jesus is with you right now, as near as the air around you and as the blood flowing within you. He is as present in your life as the light illuminating this page as you read, and as the ambient heat around you which constantly warms your body. And with Jesus, the Father and the Spirit (the same yet also different) are also in your life. He/they will be with you today, tomorrow, the day after tomorrow, and every day thereafter. Then finally, some day when all things are put right in the new heavens and new earth, it is promised, "Look! God's dwelling place is now among the people, and he will dwell with them" (Revelation 21:3). God will no, not, neither, nay, never forsake you.

As a believer in Jesus, you are not alone, and never will be for all eternity.

Pause for a moment and pray the prayer of Saint Patrick aloud. Maybe write it out on a slip of paper and keep it with you all day. Or take a picture of it with your smartphone and make it your screen photo for the day. Then every time that you look at your phone (which, as I observe people today, seems to be quite often[8]), you will be reminded of the Lord's constant and close presence in your life. The point is: find some way to remind yourself, over and over throughout the day, of Jesus' promise to love you and be present with you always.

An Appointment for Us to Keep

When Amy and I began dating, she lived in Santa Monica, California, and I about forty-five minutes away in Thousand Oaks. Because we lived so far from each other, we had to schedule our time together in advance. And as I drove to pick her up for our dates, I never once questioned whether she would be there or not. We loved each other and wanted to be together. I was confident that she would keep her word and be in the right place at the right time. There was no need to be anxious—we knew the other would keep the appointment. And there was no reason to be lonely—we had promised to be there for one another.

There is no need for you to be anxious or lonely, either. Long before you were born, Jesus looked into the future and scheduled an appointment with you for today. He determined to be with you and to love you in practical, concrete ways. As one of his disciples, he has promised to be with you always. In the Spirit he is beside you, on your right and on your left. He is in front of you and behind you, both above and below. You are completely surrounded by his presence and love. He is even within you, literally closer than any brother could be (Proverbs 18:24).

What a wonderful promise! As we pray the promises of Jesus, we begin each week, on Sunday, and focus on his promise of love and presence. As a memory aid, I suggest you memorize it this way: *It's Sunday, and I'm Surrounded by love.* Let the first two letters of Sunday be the mnemonic device that reminds you of "Su-rrounded."

As you begin your day, pray aloud the Scriptures we've looked at in this chapter, and then follow them with a simple prayer, which you can repeat over and over, all day long. Enjoy the presence of your beloved throughout the day. If you get distracted and turn away from his presence with you, don't get angry with yourself for your forgetfulness. Instead, thank him for the gentle nudge that brought him again to mind, and turn toward him once again.

Let's imagine that today is a Sunday and pray this prayer aloud:

Dear Jesus,

It's Sunday, so I'm reminded that I'm Surrounded by love.

Thank you for promising to always be present in my life, for you said, "I am with you always, even to the end of the age." Thank you for adopting and including me in the family of God.

Thank you for promising, "I am in the Father, and you are in me, and I am in you." Help me live today with the awareness that you, O God, are with me and around me and even within me.

Thank you for promising, "The one who loves me will be loved by my Father, and I too will love them and show myself to them." Allow me to feel your presence and love today, and help me remember, all day, that you will "never leave or forsake me." Because you are with me constantly, I am never alone.

In the name of the Father, and of the Son, and of the Holy Spirit. Amen.

5

Monday: I'm Making
Happiness a Habit

"A gloomy Christian is a contradiction in terms."
WILLIAM BARCLAY[1]

The average four-year-old laughs 300 times a day. The average 40-year-old? Only four."[2]

Why is it that we adults experience, on average, almost 100 percent less joy than preschoolers do? We usually assume that adults are more developed and advanced than children, which is certainly true physically and intellectually. But the opposite is true in terms of happiness. Most of us adults, if we visited a preschool class for a day, would get an *F* in joy. Let's be honest, many grown-ups are miserable at being happy. On the other hand, young children are the champions of cheer.

Maybe this is because kids live in the now, whereas many adults do not. When asked about happiness, adults often look to the future. "I'll be happy when I get married." "I'll be happy when we have children." "I'll be happy when I lose some weight." We all want to be happy, but when these milestones arrive, somehow the anticipated joy is not a part of the package.

Blaise Pascal, the brilliant sixteenth-century mathematician and philosopher, said, "All men seek happiness. This is without exception. Whatever different means they employ they all tend to this end."[3] But most of us fail to find happiness, though we all want it. The result is that, as famously put by Henry David Thoreau, "The mass of men lead lives of quiet desperation."[4]

Jesus' Promise of Joy

In contrast to Thoreau, Jesus made astonishing promises about joy:

- "I have told you this so that my joy may be in you, and that your joy may be complete" (John 15:11).

- "You will grieve, but your grief will turn to joy" (John 16:20b).

- "I will see you again and you will rejoice, and no one will take away your joy" (John 16:22b).

- "Until now you have not asked for anything in my name. Ask and you will receive, and your joy will be complete" (John 16:24).

- In prayer, Jesus said to the Father, "I am coming to you now, but I say these things while I am still in the world, so that they may have the full measure of my joy within them" (John 17:13).

Jesus also promised joy through his use of the term *blessed*. The gospel writers record him promising, about thirty times, "you will be blessed" (Luke 14:14a), and "blessed are those who have not seen and yet have believed" (John 20:29). The best-known promises of Jesus about blessing are the Beatitudes, which include promises like, "Blessed are the meek, for they will inherit the earth" (Matthew 5:5). A little known fact is that the Greek word translated "blessed" (*makarios*) could just as accurately have been rendered "happy."[5]

Some pastors and scholars quibble as to whether happy is a good translation of *makarios*, but in doing so they read the present back into the past. Their argument is based upon our contemporary view of happiness, which claims that happiness is temporary since it is based on externals that happen to us, whereas joy is lasting because it is not based on externals. Historically, however, *makarios* had little to do with what happened to a person and more to do with one's position in life.

We see this in the development of *makarios* in ancient Greek usage. Before Jesus, the chief benefactors of happiness were the elites. For the average person, life was not *makarios*. Instead, it was exceedingly difficult, full of pain, sorrow, and death. Survival was a constant struggle, and it was quite an accomplishment just to eke out food and shelter for one's family, to escape the ravages of diseases, and not to be killed in war. Daily life was a grind. This is why, for the Greeks, *makarios* originally was used only in reference to the gods. It later came to be applied to the dead who had advanced to the afterlife world of the gods, and finally to the wealthy and powerful elites of Greek society. Then, when the Hebrew version of the Old Testament was translated into Greek in the three centuries before Christ, the term was applied to those rewarded for their righteousness with luxury and riches.[6] Before Jesus, one had to be divine, dead, powerful, or have a lot of possessions in order to be happy.

Jesus then upended the whole cart, teaching that the lowly of society will be blessed in the future if they trust and follow him. Happiness was available now to every person, no matter how humble or downtrodden. Happiness was possible in spite of the externals, which is why the concept had rhetorical punch for Jesus. To say that joy is not based on externals is to miss the point; for Jesus, happiness is precisely possible for those without visible external blessings.

So Jesus made many promises about happiness and joy. If they are not synonymous, at least they are similar. When I hear someone say, "Jesus promises joy but not happiness," it always seems like splitting hairs to me. Plus, it is not only an historically dubious claim, but also etymologically unsound. Biblically speaking, the root meanings of joy convey more external action than internal attitude. For instance, the Hebrew word for joy is *gil*, which can be translated "to dance for joy" and is based on the root meaning "to spin around (under the influence of any violent emotion)."[7] But the biggest problem with this supposed division is that most people couldn't care less about whether joy and happiness are similar or different. They don't want one or the other; they want both.

Practical Prayer Pointer

When I was studying Hebrew in graduate school, I was surprised at how difficult it was to read a Hebrew phrase aloud (it was much more difficult for me than Greek or any other language had been). At first, I assumed this was because of the very different alphabet. But then I realized that all of my personal study time memorizing vocabulary and various verb endings was done in silence. I memorized the words in my head, learning to recognize them visually on the page. But when I tried to sound them out audibly in class, I struggled to piece the sounds together. Furthermore, when someone spoke a phrase, it had no connection with the figures I had memorized on paper.

This all changed when I began to study aloud, even though quietly. I found that I could memorize vocabulary lists faster, I could read faster and with more confidence, and I even began to understand more conversationally.

The same is true with prayer. Done in silence, it will take much longer to master.

Sour-Faced Christians

I believe Jesus promises us both joy and happiness. Sure, happiness seems to manifest itself as intense bursts that come and go, whereas joy is longer lasting (maybe we should call happiness "joy-moments"). Jesus wants us to be filled with joy and to exude happiness. Christians have more than enough reasons to smile rather than appear so incessantly dour. But what are we known for, our smiles or frowns?

Our culture seems to believe, hands down, that Christians are frowners and downers. Christians are seen as stern-faced, sullen party poopers. Examples of this abound. The clergyman in *The Simpsons* is Reverend Timothy Lovejoy, who not only rarely smiles but who's drooping upper lip almost makes smiling impossible. Ned Flanders, the cartoon's conservative Christian, doesn't smile much either. Reverend Shaw Moore, played by John Lithgow in the 1984 version of the movie *Footloose*, was domineering and deprecating, as was Arthur Dimmesdale in Nathaniel Hawthorne's *The Scarlet Letter*.

And this is not only the perception of Christians in fiction. The witty and wise Oliver Wendell Holmes Jr., who served thirty years as a Supreme Court justice, once confessed, "I might have entered the ministry if certain clergymen I knew had not looked and acted so much like undertakers."[8] Or as evangelist Billy Sunday quipped, "The trouble with many men is that they have got just enough religion to make them miserable. If there is not joy in religion, you've got a leak in your religion."

Is there a happiness leak in your life? If so, how can we remedy this? How can we turn the tide from joyless to joyful religion? How can we experience the promises of Jesus about joy in our daily lives? What reasons do we have to be abundantly happy?

Inexpressible and Glorious Joy

I find it fascinating that the Bible not only gives us reasons to be happy but commands it. An anonymous psalmist urged, "Sing joyfully to the LORD...shout for joy" (Psalm 33:1,3), and David insisted, "Take delight in the LORD" (Psalm 37:4). Paul insisted, "Rejoice in the Lord always. I will say it again: Rejoice!" (Philippians 4:4). And Jesus himself told his followers, "In the world you will have tribulation; but be of good cheer, I have overcome the world" (John 16:33 NKJV). In fact, Jesus' first words out of the tomb were "Take joy" (Matthew 28:9, my translation). In most versions this is rendered by the innocuous "Greetings," but the root of the command, in Greek, is simply the word "joy." I just love this: after the resurrection, Jesus' first charge could be loosely translated, "Don't worry, be happy," or even "Let's party!"

What reasons have we for such joy? First of all, joy is a character quality of God the Father ("the joy of the LORD is your strength," Nehemiah 8:10), of the Son ("I have told you this so that my joy may be in you," John 15:11a), and of the Holy Spirit ("For the kingdom of God is not a matter of eating and drinking, but of righteousness, peace and joy in the Holy Spirit," Romans 14:17). Once we grasp that joy is the very nature of God, we learn to seek the Lord of joy himself instead of merely seeking the joy of the Lord. As Irish monk Joseph Marmion put this, "Joy is the echo of God's life within us."[9]

Second, healthy believers will burst forth with the fruit of the Spirit: "For the fruit of the Spirit is love, joy..." (Galatians 5:22). Third, "a cheerful heart is good medicine" (Proverbs 17:22), and laughter has been shown clinically to be curative.[10] Fourth, salvation alone is ample reason to be continually happy. David prayed, "Restore to me the joy of your salvation" (Psalm 51:12a), and Isaiah prophesied, "With joy you will draw water from the wells of salvation" (Isaiah 12:3).

Finally, the New Testament is filled with examples of real people who experienced the reality of Jesus' joy-promises. First-century Christians were filled with "an inexpressible and glorious joy" (1 Peter 1:8), "complete joy" (1 John 1:4; 2 John 12), and "overflowing joy" (2 Corinthians 8:2). Paul said, "My joy knows no bounds" (2 Corinthians 7:4b). In these believers' lives, the joy-promises of Jesus actually came true.

An Appointment for Us to Keep

Could it be that, even today, Jesus means for these promises to come true in our lives? That he fully expects his joy to be in us, complete and full in measure, and that no one can take his joy from us?

Almost two thousand years ago, Jesus gave us, his followers, the promise of happiness; he reached out into the turbulent waters of our futures and created a new reality for our lives. I like to think of this as Jesus, long ago, scheduling a rendezvous with each of us every day, to give each of us complete and boundless joy.

I intend to keep that appointment.

I will meet Jesus today in prayer.

If Jesus plans to meet me today and give me his joy, I'll be there, ready and willing. I will enter today with great expectations—that there will be many God-given reasons for joy, many places to see his clever hand, and many occasions to be happy.

I will choose to believe that he has scheduled happiness on his calendar for me today, so I will enter his presence with singing and come into his courts with praise. I will smile, because I know he is with me, and he has delightful surprises planned for me today.

Have you ever had a day full of delightful surprises? I remember one such day clearly. On a crisp, sunny morning in January 1988, I planned an adventure for my beloved, Amy. Our senior pastor, Tim Coop, showed up at her door in chauffeur's outfit, with a rose and a clue. He then whisked her away in a white Cadillac convertible on a treasure hunt. At each location another friend awaited with a rose and a clue. Finally, she was led to a throne-like seat, set upon the top of a grassy hill.

I then came to her, riding on a white horse, dressed as a knight in shining armor. I dismounted (rather awkwardly), knelt before her, and proposed. It was a day of joy and happiness, filled with smiles and laughter. (By the way, she said yes.)

Is the Christian life likewise supposed to be a treasure hunt, planned by Jesus for us, his beloved? Has he already scheduled ways to surprise and delight us each day? If so, why are they going unnoticed? Maybe we are not paying attention. Maybe our spiritual receivers are not tuned to his frequency.

Prayer is how we tune in to his channel, and continual prayer is leaving the channel playing in the background of our hearts, as people often leave radios going in their homes or offices. And it is a choice we make, just as we can leave our radios on or off. When James, the brother of Jesus, wrote, "Consider it pure joy, my brothers and sisters, whenever you face trials of many kinds" (James 1:2), he revealed that joy is a choice. It is something we can decide to think about, something to consider.

So I choose, every Monday, to think with Jesus about joy. To look for his preplanned, hidden surprises. I will walk and talk with him nonstop today, and allow his joy to rub off on me.

I invite you to do the same. Let's begin with a prayer:

Dear Jesus,

In my mind's eye, I see you smiling and laughing. I know the Bible never describes you in that way, but I believe that is true anyway. Many of your teachings were dripping with irony and humor. Who could not laugh at a woman waking a judge, or at someone trying to remove a splinter from another person's eye while having a log in his or her own? How the common people must have smiled when you said the pompous Pharisee's prayer was unanswered or when you bested the lawyers in debate. The Bible records that the crowds heard you gladly, and that sinners liked to spend time with you.

That's what I want to do: I want to spend the day with you, Jesus. I want to smile and laugh with you and uncover, one by one, the delightful surprises you have planned for us today. Jesus, please forgive me for so often ignoring your daily presence in my life, and forgive me for allowing the sadnesses of life to eclipse the reasons to be happy.

Today, I consider it pure joy to live and breathe and walk with you.

In your name I pray. Amen.

6

Tuesday: I'm Trusting
in God's Strength

*"The Christian life is not a constant high. I have my moments
of deep discouragement. I have to go to God in prayer with
tears in my eyes, and say, 'O God, forgive me,' or 'Help me.'"*

BILLY GRAHAM[1]

It may seem odd to follow a chapter about happiness with a quote about discouragement—from Billy Graham, no less. But I want this book to be authentic, and the honest truth is that no one, living in this earthly vale of tears, is happy all the time. Sadness happens, even in the lives of mature Christians who have learned to make happiness a habit.

Martin Luther, for instance, often struggled with doubt and discouragement. He once said, "For more than a week Christ was wholly lost to me. I was shaken by desperation and blasphemy against God."[2]

Martin Luther King Jr., in a sermon preached less than a year before his assassination, said (and his congregation responded),

> I don't mind telling you this morning that sometimes I feel discouraged. (All right) I felt discouraged in Chicago. As I move through Mississippi and Georgia and Alabama, I feel discouraged. (Yes, sir) Living every day under the threat of death, I feel discouraged sometimes. Living every day under extensive criticisms, even from Negroes, I feel discouraged sometimes. [applause] Yes, sometimes I feel discouraged and feel my work's in vain. But then the Holy Spirit (Yes) revives my soul again. "There is a balm

in Gilead to make the wounded whole. There is a balm in
Gilead to heal the sin-sick soul." God bless you.[3]

Pastor and author John Piper said, "Darkness comes. In the middle
of it, the future looks blank. The temptation to quit is huge...You will
argue with yourself that there is no way forward. But with God, nothing is impossible. He has more ropes and ladders and tunnels out of pits
than you can conceive. Wait. Pray without ceasing. Hope."[4]

So take heart: if life gets you down occasionally, you are in good
company.

I am greatly encouraged that even Jesus had his times of unhappiness.
At the tomb of Lazarus, Jesus was "deeply moved in spirit and troubled,"
and as a result, the Bible simply records, "Jesus wept" (John 11:33,35). In
the Garden of Gethsemane, three of the disciples noticed that Jesus was
"deeply distressed and troubled," and Jesus even said, "My soul is over-
whelmed with sorrow to the point of death" (Mark 14:33,34). As Isaiah
had prophesied eight centuries earlier, Jesus was "a man of suffering, and
familiar with pain" (Isaiah 53:3).

In this manner, Jesus follows some of the notables of the Old Testament, for Scripture teaches that Hannah, Asaph, and Daniel were each
"deeply troubled" (1 Samuel 1:15; Psalm 73:16; Daniel 7:28). My goodness, even God the Father is "deeply troubled" at times (Genesis 6:6),
and the Holy Spirit can be grieved (Isaiah 63:10; Ephesians 4:30).

The Saddest Three Words in the Bible

The truth is that, in every human life, times of joy and sadness follow one another, almost like day and night. It may be, as dark nights
help us appreciate daylight more, so too sorrow makes us better appreciate joy. Maybe we will even more profoundly grasp the value of heavenly joy because of our earthly gasps of sorrow. The trick here on earth
is to live through sadness *hopefully*, so that joy persists even in the presence of sorrow.

This is why, if I were forced to choose the three saddest words in the
Bible, I would pick those spoken by the two disciples on the road to
Emmaus: "we had hoped" (Luke 24:21).

How very tragic. When we lose hope, we decide that the task ahead of us is impossible. We know that we lack the strength to defeat whatever foe assaults us, so we give up and throw in the towel. And when we let go of the prospect of a better tomorrow, we surrender to despair.

Let's pause for a moment and pray for those who might be discouraged or even despairing right now:

Lord,

> Somewhere today there is a man who is discouraged. I ask that you turn his heart toward you, and be to him a source of encouragement.
> Somewhere there is a woman who is feeling weak. Please remind her of her need for you, and strengthen her with your abundant power.
> Somewhere, right now, there are children or teenagers who have given up hope. I ask you to give them the gift of hope in Christ, a hope that will become the anchor for their souls.
> In Jesus' name I pray. Amen.

Jesus' Promises of Strength and Hope

But lack of strength and hope is not the end of the story for Christians; instead, it is the starting point to the Spirit-filled life. God did not intend for the Christian life to be lived on our own strength; we are to allow his strength to live in and through us. This is called the exchanged life, which has been called "the unique secret to Christianity."[5] We have been crucified with Christ, and it is no longer we who live, but Christ lives in us (Galatians 2:20). Christ is "in" us, and the Spirit "lives in" us (Romans 8:9-11). We aren't able to love, but Jesus can love through us. We can't summon the ability to forgive those who have mistreated us horribly, so Jesus forgives through us. The Spirit even prays for us when we can't summon the words (Romans 8:26). He is strong for us when we are weak. With Jesus living in and through us, there is nothing that is too difficult or impossible.

This fact is reflected in the astonishing promises Jesus made about strength:

- "Everything is possible for one who believes" (Mark 9:23).

- "Very truly I tell you, whoever believes in me will do the works I have been doing, and they will do even greater things than these, because I am going to the Father" (John 14:12).

- "Truly I tell you, if you have faith as small as a mustard seed, you can say to this mountain, 'Move from here to there,' and it will move. Nothing will be impossible for you" (Matthew 17:20-21).

- "With man this is impossible, but with God all things are possible" (Matthew 19:26).

These promises of Jesus echo the promise given centuries before through the prophet Isaiah:

> "So do not fear, for I am with you;
> do not be dismayed, for I am your God.
> I will strengthen you and help you;
> I will uphold you with my righteous right hand."
> (Isaiah 41:10)

What would our lives be like if just a few of these promises came true? What if we could tap into the power of Jesus when we feel powerless? What if we really believed that all things were possible and that we had God's strength within us?

This is exactly the experience of the apostle Paul, who wrote, "I can do all things through Him who strengthens me" (Philippians 4:13 NASB). Paul was crystal clear about the source of strength in his own life, "I thank Christ Jesus our Lord, who has given me strength" (1 Timothy 1:12), as well as in the lives of regular Christians, "But the Lord is faithful, and he will strengthen you and protect you from the evil one" (2 Thessalonians 3:3). In other words, Jesus' promise of strength is not just for apostles or super-Christians; it is for all of us, from the greatest to the least of the saints.

At times, Paul is very personal in his descriptions of receiving strength from God. To his protégé Timothy, he recalled,

> At my first defense, no one came to my support, but everyone deserted me. May it not be held against them. But the Lord stood at my side and gave me strength, so that through me the message might be fully proclaimed and all the Gentiles might hear it. And I was delivered from the lion's mouth. The Lord will rescue me from every evil attack and will bring me safely to his heavenly kingdom. To him be glory for ever and ever. Amen (2 Timothy 4:16-18).

This passage resonates with me deeply. I have often prayed, when unjustly treated or even betrayed by those I had considered friends, "May it not be held against them." And I love how Paul describes the Lord standing at his side. I find great solace in this passage when feeling discouraged or alone. In spite of my feelings, I am not alone—ever. I can do all things with Jesus at my side strengthening me.

Paul's best-known description of receiving strength concerns his "thorn in the flesh":

> Therefore, in order to keep me from becoming conceited, I was given a thorn in my flesh, a messenger of Satan, to torment me. Three times I pleaded with the Lord to take it away from me. But he said to me, "My grace is sufficient for you, for my power is made perfect in weakness." Therefore I will boast all the more gladly about my weaknesses, so that Christ's power may rest on me. That is why, for Christ's sake, I delight in weaknesses, in insults, in hardships, in persecutions, in difficulties. For when I am weak, then I am strong (2 Corinthians 12:7-10).

Here we meet the paradox of the Christian life face on: when we are weak, we are strong. When we try to succeed in our own strength, we fail. When we recognize our own powerlessness and ask for his strength to live in and through us, Jesus is faithful and keeps his promise that with God, all things are possible. This is why Paul prays in one letter, "I pray that out of his glorious riches he may strengthen you with power through his Spirit in your inner being" (Ephesians 3:16), and in a different letter he likewise prays for believers to be "strengthened with all power according to his glorious might so that you may have great endurance and patience" (Colossians 1:11).

The gifted expositor and pastor Ray C. Stedman once modestly told the story of his fear before speaking to a gathering of elites in southern California. "I felt inadequate. I felt the tremendous challenge and my own inability. I have learned, by long experience and by the Word of God, to recognize that feeling of inadequacy is an excellent thing. I welcome it now, because I know it is designed to lead me to ask for what I need."[6]

I must confess that I have not yet learned to recognize the feeling of inadequacy as an excellent thing. But the example of this older and wiser Pastor Stedman (no relation), as well as the example of Paul and other biblical heroes, encourages me to try to see my own weaknesses and frailties as opportunities for the strength of Jesus to flow through me. They are occasions when the impossible becomes possible.

Let's confess our weakness and frailties to God in prayer:

Lord,

> I want to have the confidence that I can do all things through your strength, and I want to be assured that everything is possible for those who believe.
> I pray that out of your glorious riches you would strengthen me with power through your Spirit in my inner being. I ask you to strengthen me with all power according to your glorious might so that I may have great endurance and patience. And I ask for your help to learn to recognize feelings of inadequacy as an excellent insight, a reminder to trust in you rather than myself.
> For in you, and in you alone, do I place my trust. Amen.

Are All Things Possible?

Before we conclude this discussion, I must hasten to forestall an erroneous conclusion that some Christians draw: since Jesus said "nothing will be impossible for you," it follows that all things are, indeed, absolutely possible. This mistaken conclusion ignores the evidence of Jesus' own life, and wreaks much havoc and disillusionment.

Instead, the truth is, not all things are possible. The proof of this biblically is Jesus' own prayer in the Garden of Gethsemane: "My Father, if it is not possible for this cup to be taken away unless I drink it, may your will be done" (Matthew 26:42). Obviously, for Jesus to say "if it is not possible," it must be true that he believed this particular request might, in fact, not be possible. Therefore, not all things are possible.

In some way, beyond what Jesus could feel at the moment, avoiding the cross would neither fulfill the Father's will nor glorify the Father. And since avoiding the cross was not in the Father's will, it therefore was not in the realm of possibility. Some things, though we may ask fervently and in the name of Jesus, just aren't possible. Praying is to ask when asking seems pointless, to believe when failure seems inevitable, and to know that ruin might, in fact, be God's will. As G.K. Chesterton wrote, "Hope means hoping when things are hopeless, or it is no virtue at all," and "As long as matters are really hopeful, hope is mere flattery or platitude; it is only when everything is hopeless that hope begins to be a strength."[7]

An Appointment for Us to Keep

On Tuesdays, I encourage you to concentrate on the promises of Jesus to strengthen us, to focus on the power that fills us when we pray in his name. It is not a power of our own or for our own purposes; it is his strength within us, given only to accomplish his purposes. Since we are confident of his promises and of his ability to keep them, we can move forward in faith. When we are assured that the presence of Jesus is within us, and his power is strengthening us, we are filled with hope. We may not see how our prayers might be answered, but we pray nonetheless. After all, "hope that is seen is no hope at all" (Romans 8:24), and "faith is confidence in what we hope for and assurance about what we do not see" (Hebrews 11:1). Because of the promises of Jesus, we have "hope as an anchor for the soul, firm and secure" (Hebrews 6:19), and "the hope of salvation as a helmet" (1 Thessalonians 5:8).

Does Jesus intend for these promises to come true in our lives today? I believe so. I trust that he wants to keep his appointments, with you and me today, to give us strength and hope. Believing it to be so, let's meet him in prayer:

Dear Jesus,

Dare I hope again, after so many of my hopes have been dashed on the rocks of disappointment?

Dare I believe again, even though I am filled with unbelief?

Dare I trust in your strength, when I feel so very, very weak?

Dare I step out in faith, though I often have been faithless?

Lord, I clearly cannot trust in my own wisdom to know what is best, and I cannot trust in my own strength to defeat the enemy.

So I ask you, mighty Jesus, to be my strength and my shield. I ask you to strengthen me in my inner being; strengthen my feeble arms and weak knees, and empower me and protect me from the evil one.

For you have promised that according to your will, all things are possible.

And I can do all things through you, O Christ, as you strengthen me.

I ask this in your name, which means that you would ask the same if you were physically present. Amen.

Practical Prayer Pointers

Surprise! It's time to talk about the value and importance of silent prayer. Don't let my emphasis on previous pages fool you: learning to pray silently is just as important as learning to pray aloud. One reason for this is that there are many times during the day when it is unsuitable to pray out loud. For instance, you may be standing in a checkout line at a

Walmart, and the customer in front of you is struggling with her unruly children. It would be rude to pray aloud, "Dear Jesus, help this mother with her little hellions."

Needless to say, such a prayer is at times quite needed, but it is wiser to do so in silence than out loud. For instance, I deeply appreciate people who pray for me as I preach, but I prefer that they do so in silence. Other examples might be when one is teaching a class in a public school, making a home delivery for a company, or riding on a bus or subway. All are occasions in which prayer not only may be important but crucial. "Lord, this student is struggling to understand this, so please help her grasp this new concept." "Dear Jesus, it seems to me that the people in this home are lost and in need of your love; please come into their lives and show yourself to them as the answer to all of life's problems." "O God, it seems like a fight could break out between those two commuters who are arguing. I ask you, in Jesus' name, to allow your spirit of peace to descend on them, and for this bomb to be defused."

The point is that silent prayers have their place in the Christian life also. So use and enjoy them, when appropriate.

7

Wednesday: I'm Wanting
What God Wants

*"There are only two kinds of people in the end: those
who say to God, 'Thy will be done,' and those to
whom God says, in the end, 'Thy will be done.'"*

C.S. Lewis[1]

Pleeease, can I have it? Please?"

No, this is not a four-year-old's plea to a parent. Instead, it is my summary of the vast majority of the thousands (maybe millions) of prayer requests I have read over thirty years in the ministry.

"God, would you *pleeease* help me with...?"

Many churches take a few moments during services to ask for prayer requests. I'd guess that over half the time, people ask for someone who is sick, such as, "Please pray for my grandmother who has cancer." Other common requests include financial needs, family conflicts, career issues, the return of prodigals, the salvation of certain people, and even safe travel. I'm sure you've heard a ton of these. Some are rather pedestrian, whereas others are desperate.

"Lord, *pleeease* help my new business. I need a miracle, and I need it now!"

Because our church was quite large, it was impossible to ask for verbal prayer requests during our services. So instead, almost every week I asked both members and visitors to take the prayer card out of their bulletin and write down their prayer requests. I usually said something like, "Why would anyone come to church and not write down a prayer request? Don't you know someone who is sick or in trouble or doesn't know God personally?" Week after week, there were stacks of hundreds of written requests.

"God, please bring my children back to faith in you."

"Lord, please send us more volunteers for our children's ministry."

"Dear Jesus, please protect those who are being persecuted for their faith."

"God bless the USA."

Now don't misunderstand me. I'm not suggesting these aren't perfectly valid prayers. They are, and each one is precious and important. But what I noticed, over time, is that it was very rare for someone to write, "God, I just want your will to be done," or even, "Lord, this is what I want, but if you want something different for my life, that's okay with me." Most of them were saying to God, in some manner, "God, may my will be done, *pleeease*," rather than "May your will be done."

Our Shocking Self-Confidence in Prayer

I find it odd that we Christians are so quick to assume that what we desire also happens to be precisely what God wills. How do we know he wants Grandma's cancer to be cured and isn't ready to take her home to glory? How do we know he wishes our new business to succeed, rather than grow us in humble Christlikeness through its failure? And in spite of how every politician's speech (and every country western concert) ends, how can we be sure that God wants to bless our country, instead of allow it to suffer the full measure of our sins (Genesis 15:16)? Why do we so blithely assume we have God's will figured out? I try to not assume that I always know what is best for my friends and family (though I must confess that it has been very difficult, as a father of grown kids, to let go of the assumption that I know what is best for their lives).

Come to think of it, I don't do this so consistently with anyone—except God.

The truth is that we shouldn't be so confident that our ways are God's ways. In fact, the Bible teaches the opposite. God himself says, through the prophet Isaiah, "My thoughts are not your thoughts, neither are your ways my ways" (Isaiah 55:8), and, speaking for us, says, "We all, like sheep, have gone astray, each of us has turned to our own way" (Isaiah 53:6a).

We are willful wanderers, all of us. Our default assumption is that our desires are good and right, and that we can trust our hearts to lead us. This is common advice, especially from TV gurus like Oprah and Dr. Phil. But nothing could be further from the truth. The blunt truth is that our hearts lie to us. Poets like to talk about charting our own courses and blazing our own trails, but in the end we just lead ourselves astray. In biblical terms, we deceive ourselves (1 John 1:8), we are wise in our own eyes (Isaiah 5:21), and we choose our own ways (Isaiah 65:2).

This is especially true in prayer. We naively assume that God wants what we want. We casually read, "Take delight in the LORD, and he will give you the desires of your heart" (Psalm 37:4), but we fail to notice the next verse, "Commit your way to the LORD; trust in him and he will act" (Psalm 37a, my translation). We follow the Lord's model prayer and ask, "Give us today our daily bread," but we fail to first offer, "your kingdom come, your will be done, on earth as it is in heaven" (Matthew 6:9-11).

It's All About the Name

Yet Jesus gave us very clear promises about prayer. For instance, he said,

- "You may ask me for anything in my name, and I will do it" (John 14:14).

- "You did not choose me, but I chose you and appointed you so that you might go and bear fruit—fruit that will last— and so that whatever you ask in my name the Father will give you" (John 15:16).

- "In that day you will no longer ask me anything. Very truly I tell you, my Father will give you whatever you ask in my name" (John 16:23).

- "Until now you have not asked for anything in my name. Ask and you will receive, and your joy will be complete" (John 16:24).

So how can we reconcile the fabulous promises of Jesus to grant anything we ask in prayer with the fact that our hearts tend to mislead us to desire things that may be contrary to God's will?

The answer is in the qualifier in each verse: "in the name of Jesus." We are to pray in Jesus' name.

For me, that rings a bell right away because I was raised in a church that ended every prayer, "In Jesus' name. Amen." As a child, I assumed that was the only way one should end a prayer, and probably the way Moses and David ended their prayers. To pray "in Jesus' name" was just the proper way to close off a prayer, a spiritualized "goodbye," "over and out," or "10-4." As I grew, I came to realize my error, and gradually it dawned on me that it is only one of many ways to end Christian prayer. Nonetheless, I was quite surprised when I discovered no prayer in the Bible ever ends with "in the name of Jesus. Amen." None. Zero.

Just what does it mean to "ask in the name" of Jesus, then? New Christians often wonder about the proper way to end prayer: should one say, "In Jesus' name. Amen," or "In the name of the Father, the Son, and the Holy Spirit. Amen," or what? The solution is that there is no single formula given in the Bible because the power is not in the formula but in the intent. Closing a prayer "in his name" is not a magic recipe that will suddenly make a prayer effective.

Instead, praying "in the name of Jesus" essentially means that we pray on behalf of Jesus. For instance, when a foreign ambassador speaks on behalf of a king, he speaks "in the name of" the king. An ambassador must consider, before speaking, "What would the king want if he were here in person?" This is a far cry from an ambassador who says, "I don't think the king would want this if he were here, but since I am the one in authority, I will ask for what I want." This type of request does not represent the name; it abuses the name. To pray "in the name of Jesus," therefore, is to speak what our King would say were he present.

To put this in a slightly different way, the meaning of "in his name" is to *stand in* for someone else, like an understudy in theater may stand in for the principal actor. In prayer, we take a stand for God's will to be done. This is why it is completely appropriate to pray "if it is your will."[2]

Another example might be the son of a queen who was sent to

represent her *in her stead.* Our word *instead* is derived from this very usage. So when we pray, we speak to God the Father on behalf of Jesus or in his stead.

As an aside, my surname, Stedman, may be derived from this practice. A man who stood in the place of another may have been called a "stead-man." Over time, my ancestors shortened the spelling of Steadman to Stedman, but the meaning of "stand-in" still remains. When a Christian prays in the name of Jesus, then, each one becomes a stead-man. Stead-persons, I guess, would be the politically correct way to express this.

Ray Stedman[3], the well-known pastor and author from Palo Alto, California, in the seventies and eighties, clearly understood this as the core meaning to praying in Jesus' name. In a sermon given in 1964, he said,

> To pray in Jesus' name means to stand in his place. And where was Jesus standing when he said these words? Facing the cross...Jesus knew it had to be. And to pray in Jesus' name means that you accept the process of God, the process by which he bring matters, often, to utter collapse, so that the very thing you don't want to ever happen, happens. But that is not the end of the story. Beyond it is a resurrection. Beyond it is a new beginning, a beginning of such different quality that the mind moves into an ecstasy of joy in contemplating it. That is what it means to pray in Jesus' name.[4]

This is a powerful insight: if we are standing in for Jesus, we will be facing the cross, as he was throughout his life. Our whole lives will be oriented toward the cross, so we will not be surprised by difficult situations, setbacks, or even suffering. We know for whom we stand "in stead" and how he was treated during his sojourn on earth. This is why we are encouraged, "Dear friends, do not be surprised at the fiery ordeal that has come on you to test you, as though something strange were happening to you. But rejoice inasmuch as you participate in the sufferings of Christ, so that you may be overjoyed when his glory is revealed" (1 Peter 4:12-13).

To pray "in Jesus' name," then, is not a magic phrase or secret formula. If we ask in his name, it is not a guarantee that we will get what we have asked for. As Curtis Mitchell puts this, "It's not a rabbit's foot to hang on the end of a prayer to give it punch."[5] Instead, praying in the name of Jesus is the decision to stand in for Jesus, to say and do only what he would if he were here in the flesh.

How are we to know what Jesus wants? Over time, through reading the Scriptures and abiding with Jesus, we gradually learn his preferences and desires, as long-married spouses or lifelong friends do for one another.

Truly praying "in Jesus' name" is an attitude that must permeate the entire prayer, including the ending. We say it at the end to express the spirit in which the whole prayer was uttered. Personally, I like to end my prayers with some form of Jesus' name as a reminder to me that I am praying for his will, not my own.

> Lord,
>> You have made incredible promises about prayer, including that you will do anything we ask as long as it is done in your name.
>> I understand now that this is not just a way to end prayer, but it is to be the spirit enlivening the whole prayer. I see that when I pray, I am an ambassador for you. I am standing in your place, speaking in your stead, and asking in your name.
>> So I am simply and humbly asking, as your ambassador, that your will be done, today, tomorrow, and forever.
>> Amen.

Our "Stand-In" Model

To pray in Jesus' name, then, means to pray for his will. But it is notoriously difficult to discern between his will and ours. How can I know if it is his will to take this job, buy this house, or even marry that person? How can we understand what it really means to pray for God's will rather than our own?

Once again, our Savior provides the superb example. The way Jesus lived perfectly illustrates what it means to desire the Father's will above all and how we can serve in someone else's stead. The best example of this happened in a garden called Gethsemane, which in Hebrew literally means "a press [for] oil." Knowing that betrayal, torture, and crucifixion were just ahead of him, the full weight of these sufferings bore upon Jesus. He was being hard pressed, he was being "gethsemaned" by the sufferings he knew he was about to endure.

Suddenly, the unthinkable occurred. The Son who had once said, "My food is to do the will of him who sent me and to finish his work" (John 4:34), suddenly didn't like the taste. The Immanuel who had said, "I have come down from heaven not to do my will but to do the will of him who sent me" (John 6:38), unexpectedly wanted a different assignment from his heavenly Father.

After an eternity of oneness of purpose within the Godhead, after thirty-three human years of walking in step with the Father, and after three years of teaching his disciples that he and the Father were one in being and purpose, Jesus arrived at a very uncomfortable moment. In the comfort of a garden, Jesus said what might be the most surprising words in the New Testament: "My Father, if it is possible, may this cup be taken from me" (Matthew 26:39).

For the first time in all eternity, as far as we know, the Son did not desire what the Father desired. What an incredible occurrence.

What happened to make this possible? Had there been a rift within the Trinity, a division within the One?[6] This is truly an awesome moment, one that might have caused the angelic host, as in Isaiah's day, to cover their faces and feet in astonishment and reverence (Isaiah 6:2). Richard Foster writes, "Here we have the incarnate Son praying through his tears and not receiving what he asks. Jesus knew the burden of unanswered prayer."[7] Andrew Murray, the nineteenth-century South African pastor, wrote, "For our sins, He suffered beneath the burden of that unanswered prayer."[8] What can we make of it? Were the Son and the Father at odds?

I think not, for in Mark's account, this is the only time that Jesus uttered together the words, "Abba, Father"[9] (Mark 14:36).

The Scriptures say that Jesus, in Gethsemane, "withdrew about a stone's throw beyond them, knelt down and prayed" (Luke 22:41). Why did Jesus withdraw such a distance from the disciples? Why not just a few feet or a couple of dozen? Luke goes on to record, "And being in anguish, he prayed more earnestly, and his sweat was like drops of blood falling to the ground" (Luke 22:44).

One simple answer to our question might be found in Hebrews 5:7, "During the days of Jesus' life on earth, he offered up prayers and petitions with fervent cries and tears to the one who could save him from death, and he was heard because of his reverent submission." It is very possible that in Gethsemane, Jesus removed himself a significant distance from the disciples because this prayer was not just aloud—it was really loud. I point this out just to stress that Jesus' Gethsemane prayer to the Father was probably vocalized, not silent.

Of course, there were other occasions when Jesus probably prayed silently (Luke 3:21, for instance), and we don't know how Jesus prayed when he went off by himself early in the morning or into the desert to pray (Mark 1:35; Luke 5:16). The prayer life of Jesus seemed to involve both vocalized and silent prayer, which might challenge us to grow in both types.

But "if it is possible" was not the end. Jesus finished his prayer with the fabulous "yet not my will, but yours be done" (Luke 22:42). In this moment, Jesus masterfully personified the essence of submission to the will of another, the epitome of selflessness. He chose to want what the Father wanted, to desire his desires. Jesus chose to die to self. Earlier he had said, "Truly, truly, I say to you, unless a grain of wheat falls into the earth and dies, it remains alone; but if it dies, it bears much fruit. He who loves his life loses it, and he who hates his life in this world will keep it to life eternal" (John 12:24-25 NASB). He also said, "If anyone wishes to come after Me, he must deny himself, and take up his cross daily and follow Me" (Luke 9:23 NASB). Or, as Paul put it, "I die daily" (1 Corinthians 15:31 NASB).[10]

So Jesus voluntarily died to self-will in the Garden of Gethsemane. As Foster says, "Relinquishment brings us to a priceless treasure: the crucifixion of the will."[11] Ponder this for a moment: before Jesus was crucified on the cross, his will was crucified in the garden. Maybe the garden made Calvary possible; since the crucifixion of the will had already occurred, only the crucifixion of the flesh remained. Both are, of course, extremely painful. After all, he shed blood in both places. But which was the more difficult? From this perspective, maybe Gethsemane was more challenging for Jesus than the cross.

So human will went astray in a garden called Eden and then was set straight in a garden called Gethsemane. In the first case, undefiled humans said to God, "Not your will but ours be done." In the second garden, the only remaining undefiled human said, "Not my will but yours be done."

In which garden will I choose to live today? Will I seek my will rather than God's or will I choose God's will over my own? This is especially crucial if you are in a Gethsemane right now. If so, pray this with me:

> Dear Jesus,
>
> I'm in a difficult spot again; I'm in trouble and filled with worry. I know what I would like to happen and exactly how I would like you to fix this. But I also realize how often my desires are wrongheaded and how often my solutions only lead to more trouble.
>
> So I ask for your will to be done in this situation, not mine. I want to live as you did in your Gethsemane, not as my ancestors did in Eden. Break me and mold me, shape me and form me according to your will.
>
> In your name I pray. Amen.

What Do You Do When You Find Yourself in Gethsemane?

When Jesus was confronted with a clash of wills, what did he do? Yes, he turned to prayer. He even shared with his closest friends that he was struggling and asked them to pray for him. "My soul is over-whelmed with sorrow to the point of death. Stay here and keep watch with me...Watch and pray so that you will not fall into temptation. The spirit is willing, but the flesh is weak" (Matthew 26:38,41).

Sadly, I can't say the same is often true for me. When a conflict of wills happens in my life (just ask my wife, kids, or coworkers), I usually get defensive and irritated right away. Next I get argumentative and try my best to convince my adversary that my will is more reasonable. And if none of these maneuvers work, I retreat and build an emotional wall, hoping that the silent treatment will be able to accomplish what logic and reason could not.

Trust me, Jesus' approach is much more effective than mine.

We all have our Gethsemanes. Since Jesus led his disciples into Geth-semane, it's a good bet that he will lead us into ours too. We will feel the pressure of the *geth*, the Hebrew word for "press." We will feel squeezed and pushed and even flattened by the gravity of the situation. We are the *semane*, the oil, that is being purified. In such times, what should we do?

First of all, take note that Jesus has been there before and has care-fully charted a course that we can follow. Follow his lead and pray his prayers, word for word if necessary. Next, don't assume, because you are feeling stressed and troubled, that you are in the wrong place. And don't try to find an escape hatch right away. As Jesus spent an extended time in prayer alone, resolve to stay in your Gethsemane for a while. As Jesus "knelt down and prayed" (Luke 22:41), don't be afraid if your struggles drive you to your knees. If it gets too much to bear on your knees, allow yourself to do what Jesus did: "he fell with his face to the ground and prayed" (Matthew 26:39). Today an observer might say that he fell apart and collapsed into the hands of the Father.

But most of all he prayed. "Sit here while I go over there and pray...Going a little farther, he fell with his face to the ground and prayed...He went away a second time and prayed" (Matthew 26:36,39,42). Both Mark and Luke express the same theme: "he fell to the ground and prayed...once more he went away and prayed...he prayed more earnestly, and his sweat was like drops of blood falling to the ground" (Mark 14:35,39; Luke 22:44). As theologian and author

N.T. Wright quipped, "Gethsemane is the place which reminds us that the real battle must be won on our knees in advance."[12]

An Appointment to Keep

Rather than wait for a crisis to drive me into Gethsemane, I like to make each Wednesday a Gethsemane, an appointment in the garden with Jesus. I thoroughly enjoy praying for his will to be done in my life. Even more, I pray that I would grow to want what he wants. To thirst after his ways. To hunger for his righteousness. As Jesus said, "Blessed are those who hunger and thirst for righteousness, for they will be filled" (Matthew 5:6).

I also enjoy praying this for my family, friends, and the members of our church. For some reason, though, I especially like praying this for my kids. They are all young adults now, launching out on their own journeys. But will they seek their own will or God's? Will they continue to believe that God knows best and that the Bible fully reveals his will for their lives? Or will they succumb to peer pressure, decide that the Bible is old-fashioned and out of date, and feel free to pick and choose the teachings of Jesus that best align with their own motives? Who will pray for them, fervently and regularly, that they choose to follow the pattern of Jesus and pray, "Not my will, but yours be done"?

I consider this my parental privilege, my fatherly duty, every Wednesday. I pray for their hearts to align with God's.

During a trip to China in 1947, Bob Pierce was moved to compassion for the destitute children he saw. As a result, he wrote a simple prayer in the flyleaf of his Bible, "Let my heart be broken with the things that break your heart." Because of this prayer, Bob founded World Vision International in 1950 and Samaritan's Purse in 1970, two of the largest charitable organizations in the world today.[13] His prayer is a modern way of asking for God's will rather than our own. Let's pray this right now:

> Lord,
>
> I want, above all else, for your will to be done in my life and in this world, but I often get confused and my will gets in the way. So today I sincerely ask that your will, not mine, be done.

In the spirit of Bob Pierce, I also pray for those I love:

Lord, let their hearts be broken with the things that break your heart.

Let their minds be filled with the thoughts that fill your mind.

Let their emotions be moved by the feelings that fill your soul.

Let their values be based on what you have determined is right.

Let their delights be aligned with what you find delightful.

Let their futures unfold along the paths you have planned for them.

Let their lives bring you glory as you always sought to glorify the Father.

Jesus, I pray this in your name, in your stead. Amen.

8

Thursday: I'm Trading My
Troubles for Peace

"'Come hither to me, all ye that labour and are heavy laden, I
will give you rest.' Oh! Wonderful, wonderful! That the one
who has help to give is the one who says, 'Come hither'!"

Soren Kierkegaard[1]

Do you control your worries or do your worries control you?

For most of us, we tend toward the latter. Worry is seen as a feeling that we cannot control or schedule; it arises suddenly and sullenly, taking over our thoughts and emotions. Worry is a virus that worms its way into our minds. It's a bully on the playground of our hearts that threatens our sense of safety. It's a terrorist that takes our helpless thoughts hostage.

But are we really helpless, or is worry something we can conquer?

My answer is the latter. Take, for instance, the charming case of the British industrialist, filmmaker, and Christian, Baron J. Arthur Rank. His many worries brought on painful ulcers and, quite remarkably, drove him to a brilliant solution: he decided to worry only on Wednesdays. On other days of the week, if anything caused him to worry or be anxious, he wrote it down and placed the paper in his "worry box" to be dealt with on a later date. What Rank found when he opened the box each Wednesday, however, was that most of his concerns somehow had already been resolved. By compartmentalizing and delaying his worries to a later date, Rank found a way to successfully control anxiety.

This is good news. If Baron Rank could do it, so can we.

In addition, defeating worry must be possible, because Jesus commanded that very thing. In the Gospels, "do not worry" drops from Jesus' lips nine times.[2] I wonder, is there any command of Jesus that we modern Christians ignore and violate more?

Lord,

> Is it possible to live without worry? To be free from anxiety?
> When I read in your Word the command, "Do not worry,"
>   I confess that I disobey this command often; it seems
>   impossible to obey, like "Do not breathe." Yet you are
>   the Lord of the possible, the God who can do anything,
>   and I know that nothing is too difficult for you.
> And I see in your life, Jesus, when you walked upon the
>   Earth, that you did not fret or fuss, and you didn't fill
>   your mind with "what ifs." Instead, you lived each day
>   in confident assurance that the Father's will was good
>   and perfect. Even though you had the weight of the
>   world upon your shoulders, you lived free of worry and
>   fear.
> So I ask you today to help me learn to be more like you,
>   Jesus. Help me discover how to not worry about any-
>   thing, and instead to pray about everything. Help me
>   to pray with thanksgiving, so the peace of God that sur-
>   passes understanding may fill my heart and mind as I
>   trust in you.
> In the worry-free name of Jesus I pray. Amen.

Worry Is a Choice

Since Jesus commanded us to not worry, we must have the capacity to obey. His command suggests we have both the ability and the tools necessary to get the job done. It must be an option we can either choose or reject. Thus, worry is a choice that we make, not a condition that is forced on us. There are no worry-victims, only worry-choosers.

But this is easier said than done. In my own life, I have struggled mightily at times with the worries and stresses that mount in a church of several thousand. I worried about people's feelings and church finances, and I worried when conflict raised its ugly head. I worried about whether the music was too loud or too soft, and I worried when it rained or when it was too hot on weekends. I worried about whether our members were really growing into Christlikeness, and I worried that they never would do so with someone like me as their leader.[3] And then I worried that, as the senior pastor, I shouldn't worry so much.

In hindsight, I now realize that most of my worries were unnecessary; God's grace was more than sufficient, and our church was blessed abundantly. As philosopher Michel de Montaigne said, "My life has been full of terrible misfortunes, most of which have never happened."[4] Nonetheless, worry was an enemy I had to learn how to defeat.

In my own journey of faith, two spiritual disciplines help me conquer worry. The first is simply to change *to whom* I worry. I have learned to defeat worry by replacing worrying *to myself* with worrying *to God*. In this way, worry becomes prayer and recurring worries become unceasing prayers. In short, the first secret is to turn our fretting into praying.

The second is to specify one day each week to trade our troubles for peace. This is why I love praying the promises of Jesus on Thursdays. On this day of the week, I focus on the promises of Jesus about peace and rest.[5]

Jesus' Promises of Peace and Rest

Is a life of peace and rest possible? Since Jesus has given us these very great and precious pledges, the answer is a resounding yes.

- "Come to me, all you who are weary and burdened, and I will give you rest. Take my yoke upon you and learn from me, for I am gentle and humble in heart, and you will find rest for your souls. For my yoke is easy and my burden is light" (Matthew 11:28-30).

- "Peace I leave with you; my peace I give you" (John 14:27).

- "I have told you these things, so that in me you may have peace. In this world you will have trouble. But take heart! I have overcome the world" (John 16:33).

In these great and precious promises, our Lord reaches out into the future to positively influence the lives of his followers—you and me. In a world filled with trouble, he has destined for us to be at peace. In cultures overrun with stress and anxiety, he has prearranged for us to find rest. Jesus desires to meet us today, in the midst of our troubles, and give us peace. The question is: will we keep that appointment?

Peace is a popular subject in the Bible. In the wilderness, God's promise to the Israelites was called a "covenant of peace" (Numbers 25:12). In the Psalms, the Lord "blesses his people with peace" and "he promises peace to his people" (Psalm 29:11; 85:8). In a lovely analogy about the future, he writes, "righteousness and peace kiss each other" (Psalm 85:10). Solomon teaches there is "a time for war and a time for peace" (Ecclesiastes 3:8), and the prophets repeatedly promise "you will have peace" (Jeremiah 30:10; 46:27).

But as the time nears for the Messiah to be born, peace becomes not merely something he brings but an aspect of his very being. Micah says of the one to be born in Bethlehem, "he will be our peace" (Micah 5:2,5), and Isaiah reveals his very title will be "Prince of Peace" (Isaiah 9:6). As a result, Paul is able to teach about Jesus in the New Testament, "he himself is our peace" (Ephesians 2:14), "let the peace of Christ rule in your hearts" (Colossians 3:15), and "may the Lord of peace himself give you peace at all times and in every way" (2 Thessalonians 3:16).

This is why I suggested in *Praying the Armor of God* (the companion volume to this book) that the "shoes of peace" signified not just some vague notion of conflict resolution, but instead the very peace of Christ and thus the presence of Christ himself in our lives.[6] Peace is not just a blessing Jesus brings with him, but it is part of the essence he is within himself. Peace is a part of Jesus' person, not just his personality. To put this in a different way, a non-Christian cannot simply put on the shoes of peace; one can only put on Christ, that is, be clothed with Christ (Galatians 3:27). When we do that, suddenly our feet are well shod. When the Prince of Peace comes into our lives, peace is a part of the package.

Practical Prayer Pointers

For those who have read my book *Praying the Armor of God*, at first glance it might seem confusing to pray both the armor and the promises of Jesus. In actual practice, I have found them to be neither conflicting nor confusing. Instead, my prayer life has been enriched by a new theme I can integrate into my daily practices.

Personally, I like both continuity and variability in my prayers. So I still pray the armor of God daily, and use the day of the week to focus my prayers for the day. On Mondays I ask God to Make fast the breastplate of righteousness and on Thursdays to help us Think within the helmet of salvation, and so on. After memorizing the promises of Jesus, it was very easy to integrate them into my prayers throughout each day. Thus, on Mondays I also take time to Make happiness a habit and on Thursdays I pray to Trade my troubles for peace. (And as a preview to a future book in this series, I also thoroughly enjoy praying the fruit of the Spirit in this manner.)

Come to Me and I Will Give You…Yoga?

Sadly, our postmodern world completely misses this truth about Jesus. They see Christians as burdened rather than burden-free, and they assume that Christianity brings guilt rather than peace. But the thirst for personal peace is deeply implanted in the human heart. When Elvis was asked what money can't buy, he said, "Peace." The actor Harrison Ford, after he said, "You only want what you ain't got," was asked what he wanted. His one-word reply, "Peace."

So people today recognize the need for peace, but they search for it everywhere but in the Prince of Peace himself. To adapt the words of an old song, they are looking for peace in all the wrong places. They grasp after any solution offered except, strangely, by the Savior himself.

In Jesus' day, deeply troubled people came to him, but never once did Jesus say, "Here's an herb to dull the pain." (In fact, at the crucifixion Jesus was offered a pain reliever to lessen his suffering, but he refused.[7]) He never advocated yoga for stress management nor suggested an eastern religion meditation to remove oneself from the sufferings of life.

So what was Jesus' grand solution for those who were burdened and troubled? Jesus' shocking solution: himself! Jesus separated himself from all other spiritual guides and religions with this jaw-dropping claim: "Come to me…I will give you rest."

What an astonishing claim.

Siddhartha never said, "Come to me...I will solve your problems." Neither did Muhammad, the Hindu yogis, nor any new age spiritualists today. All other religions said, "Do this or that." Jesus alone said, "I will do it all."

For Christians, it's all about him.

Flip back a few paragraphs and reread the bulleted promises of Jesus. Notice that the words repeated most often are neither *peace* nor *rest*; instead, they are the first person pronouns *I, me, my*. Jesus refers to himself thirteen times in five verses.

Jesus himself, not merely a Jesus-like lifestyle, is the solution to worry, stress, and trouble. The cure for anxiety is not just to follow Jesus' way of life, but to be filled with Jesus himself. He is our peace. His peace he will give us. He will give us rest.

So if peace is part of the package, why do so many Christians worry and fret? Why are we believers so often bereft of peace? How do we begin to experience the peace of Jesus in a real and tangible way?

Lord,

> Why is this true about me? Why am I so filled with worries, even though I am a Christian? Why am I so fearful, even though I know you are with me? Help me to discover the path to peace and rest, because somehow, somewhere, I seem to have lost the directions.
>
> Thank you. Amen.

Three Steps to Experiencing Rest and Peace

How can the promise of peace and rest become real in our lives today? Jesus himself outlined three steps in this process, expressed by three separate commands: "Come to me, all you who are weary and burdened, and I will give you rest. Take my yoke upon you and learn from me, for I am gentle and humble in heart, and you will find rest for your souls. For my yoke is easy and my burden is light" (Matthew 11:28-30).

The first step is to *come to Jesus*. In the Greek language, "Come to me" is actually a command. Jesus does not beg us to follow him, he orders. This is the most important summons ever offered to human beings: come to Jesus Christ as Savior and Lord. What a grand invitation this is. Were you or I to receive an invitation from the president of the United States that said, "Come to visit me at the White House," we would be overjoyed. Such a meeting might be the highlight of our lives, the story we told and retold to our children and grandchildren.

Before us is an invitation of even grander magnitude and importance. We are invited into the presence of the living God, and we can "approach God's throne of grace with confidence, so that we may receive mercy and find grace to help us in our time of need" (Hebrews 4:16). Plus, this invitation is not for a one-hour visit. It is to become a permanent part of his family and to dwell with him eternally. Our new address is even better than 1600 Pennsylvania Avenue. We are "seated with him in the heavenly realms" (Ephesians 2:6).

I assume that most readers have already responded to this invitation, and count themselves as followers of Jesus. If you have yet to do this, don't wait another moment. Bow in prayer, and humbly ask Jesus to be your Lord and Savior.

Dear Jesus,

I'm amazed that you would offer to love and forgive me, because I've made so many mistakes in my life and I have hurt so many people. I've pretty much made a mess of things. I realize that if heaven is a perfect place, then I have disqualified myself from entering there.

But I have been told that you are a gracious and loving Savior who will forgive and cleanse me if I will believe and follow you. So I come to you today, confessing that I am a sinner and repenting of my past. I ask you, Jesus, to be the Lord and Savior of my life, and I pledge to live the rest of my life for you.

In your name I pray. Amen.

Note that Jesus bids us to come to him, not to a certain church or to a particular denomination. He didn't invite us to become religious or otherworldly. He didn't ask us to be a part of an organization; we are to be a part of him. How do we do this?

The answer is in the second command, "Take my yoke." A yoke was a harness used to connect two oxen, and it was usually made of a large plank of wood with two holes for the oxen's heads. When yoked together, the two animals were forced to move together in the same direction at the same pace. They literally had no choice but to walk together.

In the same way, when we obey Jesus' command to "take my yoke," we tie ourselves irrevocably to Jesus and begin to walk with him throughout life. We must walk together, as contestants do in a three-legged race. This is why I call the second step to find real peace and rest: *walk with Jesus*.

When Jesus called his first disciples, he said, "Come, follow me" (Matthew 4:19) and—incredibly—several men actually dropped their nets and started to walk with him. (I'm unsure if I would have done the same, to be honest.) And for the next three years, they walked...and walked...and walked. They arose together in the morning with Jesus, ate and drank with him, walked alongside him, and then slept near him at night, wherever he chose to lay his head. They spent time with Jesus, traveled wherever he went, and seem to have talked much of the time. As Enoch walked with God before the flood (Genesis 5:22), and as Moses talked with God as a friend (Exodus 33:11), so a small band of disciples walked and talked with God-in-the-flesh, Jesus.

Wouldn't it have been fabulous to walk with Jesus? To talk with him, listen to his teaching, and watch him closely? Today we believers can do the same through the presence of Jesus in the Holy Spirit and through his voice in the Scriptures. Jesus explained this marvelous truth, saying, "I will not leave you as orphans; I will come to you. Before long, the world will not see me anymore, but you will see me. Because I live, you also will live. On that day you will realize that I am in my Father, and you are in me, and I am with you...But very truly I tell you, it is for your good that I am going away" (John 14:18-20; 16:7).

Occasionally I have heard Christians say something like, "I wish Jesus were here with us personally, as he was in the flesh two thousand years ago." Well, it is a good thing for everyone else that he does not grant that wish, because he would then be unavailable for others. During Jesus' life on earth, he was limited by the laws of physics to be in one place at one time, so he could walk with only a limited number of people. But now that Jesus has ascended to heaven, he is able to be with billions of followers at once. He is with each of us and in us by the power of the Spirit.

Jesus called this "abiding." He said, "Abide in me, and I in you" (John 15:4 NASB). Paul put it this way, "Christ lives in me" (Galatians 2:20). This is a massively important truth, which I will cover in depth in a future book in this series. For now, it must suffice for us to understand that "abide" basically means to reside or dwell with someone, but it means much more than just sharing a common house or dwelling. It means to share life with another person, to "do life" together. It means to walk closely together throughout life.

To abide with Jesus, then, is to commit to walking with and sharing life with him, every moment of the day. In practical terms, it means believing that Jesus is with us at all times. It is enjoying his constant presence and ongoing communication with him. The Christian life is taking a long walk with Jesus, all day, each and every day. And with Jesus at our side, fears and unrest seem to vanish. If he is so calm and collected, well, then I can be the same.

At this point we pass naturally onto the third step of the peace process: *learn from Jesus*. This also was his command, for he said, "Learn from me." In time, we begin to take on his cadence and gait, and learn to automatically walk in step with him. We learn to walk not just with him but like him.

During this phase, we especially learn the habits of gentleness and humility, because Jesus himself specified them: "Take my yoke upon you and learn from me, for I am gentle and humble in heart" (Matthew 11:29).

We learn that both gentleness and humility are choices, just as worry was, for they too are commanded of us. Paul wrote, "Be completely humble and gentle" (Ephesians 4:2), and "Let your gentleness be evident to all" (Philippians 4:5). But don't assume that gentleness is the same as weakness. The opposite is the case. When two oxen were connected together, their strength was increased exponentially. If either ox could pull a quarter-ton cart alone, together they might pull not just a half-ton, but three-quarters or even a full ton.

It is the same in our case with Jesus, but quite lopsided. We are able to pull just a bit, whereas he can move mountains. It is like Jack Haley, the NBA basketball player who celebrated after a Chicago Bulls game, saying, "One day I'll be able to tell my grandchildren that Michael Jordan and I scored fifty-one points together," knowing that Jordan had scored fifty of them. The point is, when we are yoked with Jesus, there really isn't anything that we can't do together. This is why Paul was able to exclaim, "I can do everything through Christ, who gives me strength" (Philippians 4:13 NLT).

And humility is also a choice.

> All of you, clothe yourselves with humility toward one
> another, because,
>
> > "God opposes the proud
> > but gives grace to the humble."
>
> Humble yourselves, therefore, under God's mighty hand,
> that he may lift you up in due time. Cast all your anxiety
> on him because he cares for you (1 Peter 5:5b-7).

This last verse sums up this whole topic nicely. Those of us who are weary and heavily burdened can come to Jesus and give him our burdens. Jesus cares for us. He desires to help us and wants to carry our burdens. We merely have to lay them down.

I'm reminded of the story of a man who one night asked God in prayer, "Lord, I'm so terribly troubled and overwhelmed, so I gave you all my burdens. Why don't I feel better?" God simply replied, "You haven't let go of them yet."

An Appointment to Keep

How do we let go? How do we trade our troubles for peace?

By this point in the book, I'm sure you already know the answer: we let go of our burdens in prayer. I learned this early in my Christian walk, since this verse was the first one I memorized: "Do not be anxious about anything, but in every situation, by prayer and petition, with thanksgiving, present your requests to God. And the peace of God, which transcends all understanding, will guard your hearts and your minds in Christ Jesus" (Philippians 4:6-7).

In fact, let's not just read this—let's pray it:

Dear Jesus,

I choose to come to you today and give you my burdens, concerns, and fears. I come before you with thanksgiving, aware of the many undeserved blessings in my life. I come with prayers and petitions, asking you to relieve me of my worries and burdens. I take your yoke upon me and choose to walk with you the rest of my life. I pledge to learn from you as we walk together. I want to adopt your pace and style, and learn when to pause or hurry, when to listen or speak, and where to find peace and rest.

I rest today in your name and will. Amen.

9

Friday: I'm Finding Freedom

*"Whenever I hear anyone arguing for slavery, I feel a
strong impulse to see it tried on him personally."*
ABRAHAM LINCOLN[1]

Let's start with a quick Bible quiz:

What are the first words in the Bible that God spoke to Adam?

1. Hi Adam. This is God speaking.

2. Take care of my garden.

3. Be fruitful and multiply.

4. She's pretty neat, isn't she?

5. It's not good to be alone.

6. None of the above.

If you chose number six, you are correct. The first three words spoken by God to Adam were: "You are free" (Genesis 2:16).[2]

For me, this fact is astounding and unexpected. God's first words to humans in the Bible were not, "Welcome to the world," "I love you," or "You must obey me." They also weren't, "You must worship me" or "You need to attend church once a week." Instead, God's initial words were, "You are free to eat from any tree in the garden."

This is more than a mere explanation of the garden menu—this is a declaration from the very beginning that humans have free will. We are not biological automatons or robots. Human choice is a real thing. Freedom was God's original intention. Adam was, as the song goes, "Born

Free" (just to be clear, I'm referring to the song by Andy Williams, not Kid Rock or M.I.A.).

Free Will Is Impossible Without Limits

Into this perfect paradise, God gave Adam only one limit. Jews have 613 laws to keep in the Torah, and Moses gave ten commandments in Exodus. But Adam had only one measly law to follow, and it wasn't even a difficult one. If Adam were alive today, the modern-day equivalent might go something like this: "Adam, you can drive this Porsche as long as you want and anywhere you want. Plus, you can listen to any station on the radio. Except, that is, this one rule: you can't listen to station XYZ." And what does Adam do? He gets in the car and almost immediately, it seems, turns to station XYZ. It's nuts.

Would you be so foolish? If someone said to you, "From now on, all of the entrées at your favorite restaurant will be free for you and your family. It's all-you-can-eat, at no cost—forever. There's only one catch: there is one item you can't order. If you order that one forbidden entrée, you get nothing and you get kicked out of our restaurant forever." Now think about it: great meals, for free and forever, or one meal and you are booted out. What would you do?

Why on earth did Adam and Eve choose the latter?

And why would God set up such a trivial condition? Has it ever seemed arbitrary to you that God would single out one tree, which was both beautiful to look at and good for food (Genesis 3:6)? It wasn't poisonous or bad tasting; in fact, it was the opposite. Why that one tree?

Furthermore, why would God do this when he knew, in his divine foreknowledge, that they would fall? And what happened when Eve ate the fruit? Nothing physiologically occurred, or so it seems. "Then the eyes of both of them were opened" (Genesis 3:7) clearly referred not to physical sight but to moral perception.

Why did God give them this one apparently random law?

Because they needed boundaries—at least one—to be truly free. The exceptions are what make freedom possible. "You must not eat" was God's way of saying, "You are not gods and you need limits." As Cicero said: "We are in bondage to the Law in order that we may be free."

John Steinbeck (of all people) understood this clear meaning in the Hebrew text. He wrote, "But [it is] the Hebrew word, the word *timshel*— 'Thou mayest'—that gives a choice. It might be the most important word in the world. That says the way is open. That throws it right back on a man. For if 'Thou mayest'—it is also true that 'Thou mayest not.'"[3]

God knew we needed limits and rules to be human, because we are not omniscient know-it-alls. Only God himself is without limitations. He can do anything and knows everything. Simply put, humans needed to grasp from the start that they were not divine, there were limitations to their understanding, and the best way to live was to follow God's instructions.

Lord,

> Why did Adam and Eve eat the forbidden fruit and start the human race down such a devastating path? I wonder—would I have done the same had I been one of the first humans created?
>
> Well, there is no need to consider that question very long, because every day I choose to think thoughts and sport attitudes that I know are against your will. I am no better than Adam or Eve; no wiser or stronger than they. So help me understand why they ate from that prohibited tree and in doing so, better understand why I do the same today. Help me learn to love the limits you have set on my life and to enjoy both the freedoms and boundaries you have given.

In Jesus' name. Amen.

Practical Prayer Pointers

I have mentioned previously that learning to talk with God is similar to learning to talk any language: the best way to rapidly improve is to practice speaking aloud with someone who is fluent in that language. So how can this work regarding talking with God since he is so frustratingly silent? Well, actually he has spoken to us in the Scriptures, and we can learn to pray by speaking his words back to him. And some of his best words, which we can to learn to speak, are his promises. As the saints of old often said, we are to learn to "plead the promises," which simply means that we are to ask God to be faithful to the promises he has already made.

When God told Adam, "You are free to eat," he revealed that Adam had choices. But it was when God followed that clause with "except..." that God revealed to Adam that he had more than bestial freedom; Adam had moral freedom, which is what made him human and distinct from animals. We humans have the ability to make moral choices and are not driven by instinct and impulse alone.

A beast in the Garden of Eden would also be able to make choices, albeit rudimentary ones. Eat this leaf, then that flower, and so forth. But God never said to an animal, "No, I said leave that flower alone." God set no limitations upon the beasts, and they were left to learn only through trial and error. Why?

The limitations are what make us human.

The boundaries cause a choice to take on moral dimensions. This is why God said to Adam, "You are free to eat from any tree in the garden; but you must not eat from the tree of the knowledge of good and evil, for when you eat from it you will certainly die" (Genesis 2:16-17).

The Freedom to Love

As psychologists understand, clear boundaries are essential to health. Kids need rules and boundaries to be safe and to know they are loved. Without limitations, kids grow up feeling the world is a chaotic and unsafe place. They become fearful and view others as unreliable. [4]

Good parents, on the other hand, communicate safety and reliability through boundaries. Parents say to preschoolers: "You are free to play in our yard, but you can't play in the street." Is this because the parents are mean and petty? No, they give their kids boundaries because they love them.

"You have to eat your dinner or no dessert." "You must make your bed before you come down for breakfast." "Wash your hands after you use the bathroom." Parents give these and a million other directives before most children even can understand the reasons behind the rules. In this light, the one parameter God gave Adam seems mild and manageable.

Parents also give their children what might appear to be arbitrary rules, just as God's rule might have seemed to Adam and Eve. Is there any person alive who, during childhood, didn't hear from a parent, "Because I said so"? No reason, no explanation. Just do it.

In other words, boundaries make love possible.

When we choose to love, we also choose whom we will not love. When I chose Amy to be my wife and vowed to be her faithful husband, I also chose that I would not love any other woman on earth in the same way. When she and I chose to be parents, we chose to love our children in a way that was exclusively different from how we would treat other children. When we chose to become members of a church, we chose where we will be and where we would not be on most Sundays.

Free love always involves limitations, which is why our culture massively misunderstands both freedom and love.

The average person-on-the-street, if asked to define freedom, might say something like, "Freedom is the ability to do my own thing, free from the control of others," or "Freedom is to be my own boss, free from all limitations or guidelines." Freedom, put in this light, is to be free from authority, from responsibility, or from restrictions. Do you notice the common word? *From.* Our modern notion is that freedom is *from* something.

And what about "free love"? Is there any phrase more misunderstood? Lynyrd Skynyrd sang "Free Bird," and Steven Stills wrote "Love the One You're With" (in my opinion, the dumbest song ever written). In both cases, they were putting to music the false premise of fallen humanity: real love has no limitations.

The exact opposite is the truth. There is no real love without limitations. There is no "You are free" without "but you must not."

Freedom, just like promises, always involves limits. If I were to promise to meet you at our church at 6:00 p.m. next Tuesday, this commitment limits my choices for 6:00 p.m. next Tuesday. When a person takes a job, she severely limits where she can be during work hours. When one decides to go on a diet to lose weight and be healthier, it limits what or how much one can eat.

This is especially true about love. I know of a single man who said to a woman at church, "God told me to marry you." He was very surprised when this did not impress her. When he asked me about it, I asked him, "Do you think she felt loved by you?"

He responded, "What do you mean? I asked her to be my wife."

"No you didn't. You told her God was asking her to be your wife. She wants to do God's will, but she also wants someone to choose her— freely choose her."

He walked away, shaking his head and saying, "I'll never understand women."

No, what he didn't understand was the nature of love. Or free will. Or promises. They all go together. Without free will, love is impossible.

This is why God said to Adam, "You are free...but you must not." God was readying Adam for Eve, teaching him how to love. Illustrating that love involves limits, and if you love others, you will respect their requests, even when you don't fully understand them. God was training Adam to be a good husband and father, teaching him that true freedom always includes boundaries. Tragically, Adam failed the exam, and in doing so traded freedom for slavery.

Jesus' Promises About Freedom

When Jesus lived, Rome ruled the world. Rome was the colossus with massive power and wealth; Jesus, from an earthly point of view, had neither. Yet he had the audacity to make these colossal promises:

- "If you hold to my teaching, you are really my disciples. Then you will know the truth, and the truth will set you free" (John 8:31-32).

- "If the Son sets you free, you will be free indeed" (John 8:36).

- "The Spirit of the Lord is on me, because he has anointed me to proclaim good news to the poor. He has sent me to proclaim freedom for the prisoners and recovery of sight for the blind, to set the oppressed free, to proclaim the year of the Lord's favor" (Luke 4:18-19).

Because of these great and precious promises, freedom in Christ is a recurring theme in the rest of the New Testament. We have been "set free from sin" (Romans 6:18), and we have been "called to be free" (Galatians 5:13).

My favorite verse in the whole Bible is about freedom: "It is for freedom that Christ has set us free. Stand firm, then, and do not let yourselves be burdened again by a yoke of slavery" (Galatians 5:1).

This is the promise of Christ to you: to set you free. Not merely "set free from" but "set free for." Specifically, we have been set free for freedom!

He spoke it before you were born, but he had you in mind. "You will know the truth, and the truth will set you free" (John 8:32).

He knew you would be harassed and deceived by Satan. He realized you would be tempted beyond your own ability to withstand. He understood you would be ensnared and enslaved by sin and evil.

Even so, Jesus came to set you free.

He uttered the words two thousand years ago, but fully meant for them to powerfully apply today. He reached into your future to do what you could not do: release yourself from bondage to evil.

Jesus came to set you free. I know I'm repeating myself, but we need to let this sink in. Say it—and pray it—over and over: "Set free, set free, Jesus has set me free."

In the words of Martin Luther King Jr., "Free at last, free at last, thank God Almighty, we are free at last."[5]

A Way Out of the Confusion

It's not easy being free. As the humorist Will Rogers quipped, "Liberty doesn't work as well in practice as it does in speeches."[6] This is especially evident in the current clash of liberties in our world today. Our culture is now enslaved to license, so much so that it is unable to decide even basic moral issues. For instance, which is more important: the freedom of a mother over her own body or the freedom of the preborn child to live? The freedom of speech or the protection against bullying or hateful words? The freedom of religious business owners to not violate their own conscience, or the freedom of a customer to not be discriminated against? The freedom of a cartoonist to draw a picture of Muhammad, or the rights of a religious zealot who is offended by such a cartoon?

Today massive confusion exists over whose rights ought to prevail. It seems like the most vocal, well-funded, or even violent groups are winning the day. How can we hope to achieve freedom when our very ideas about freedom collide?

We also struggle with freedom on a more personal basis. Adults are free to smoke and drink, but these freedoms often lead to addictions, which is a form of chemical slavery. We are free to be sexually uninhibited, but not free from the infectious and moral cost of such behavior. We are free from sexism and patriarchy, but confused about what gender identity means. We are free to divorce, but not free from the tragic consequences of family breakups.

In our quest for freedom, we have made a mess of things.

What is the solution to our predicament? The answer, once again, is prayer. We cannot do this ourselves, but we can, with confidence, ask God to do this. We know this is his will, because of Jesus' promises about freedom.

The solution to the ills of our world is for each of us to live in constant communion and conversation with God and to learn that freedom is found in binding ourselves to Christ. Then it is praying for such freedom to become a reality in our lives, the lives of others, the whole world—and even the cosmos.

I am learning to dedicate Fridays to this discipline, and I encourage you to do the same.

Each Friday morning I try to begin my day with my mind and heart focused on the promises of Jesus for freedom. I pray them over and over, asking him to make their truth become more and more apparent in my life. Then all day long I revel in the freedom that is ours in Christ. Freedom from sin and selfishness, and liberty from condemnation and death. "There is now no condemnation for those who are in Christ Jesus" (Romans 8:1).

This is the hope of the world. Thomas Jefferson wrote, in a flash of theological insight, "We hold these truths to be self-evident, that all men are created equal, that they are endowed by their Creator with certain unalienable Rights, that among these are Life, Liberty and the pursuit of Happiness." The Declaration of Independence is based on a biblical understanding: God created humans to be free.

Upon this foundation, America became a beacon of freedom to the world; without it, the quest for liberty slowly crumbles. So, may we today embrace both free will and boundaries, love and limits, and experience life as God originally intended.

As we close this chapter, read the following prayer aloud, expanding or adjusting it to the names and needs of those in your life, and pausing in the places where you sense God may want you to linger. Pray for true freedom in your life and in the lives of your family members, friends, church community, our nation, and the world.

Dear Jesus,

You said the truth would set me free, so I ask you today for that promise to become true in my life. I ask you also to do the same for those I care about. I pray that your love would set my spouse (or friends) free to be the person she/he was created to be. I pray that your truth would fill my children's (or my relatives' children's) minds, and it would set them free to follow the paths of righteousness all the days of their lives.

I pray for my extended family and friends, that they might experience the love and freedom of the gospel in new and transformational ways. I pray for our church family to be a community free to love like Christ and free from legalism, which robs us of life and joy. And I pray that our nation and the whole world might understand that true freedom and love are not found in denying your existence, God, but in embracing you.

I pray for myself and my struggles with addictions, and I ask you, O God, to set me free. I pray the same for my family, friends, and others who are in bondage to some stronghold of the evil one.

Finally, I pray for those Christians around the world who

are suffering physical persecution and possibly even
incarceration; I ask you to free them from their chains.
You have promised to proclaim freedom for prisoners
and to set the oppressed free.

May these promises become reality today, according to
your name and glory. Amen.

10

Saturday: I'm So Excited
About Heaven

*"If I find in myself a desire which no experience in
this world can satisfy, the most probable explanation
is that I was made for another world."*

C.S. Lewis[1]

Several years ago, the surprise TV hit of the year was *Extreme Make-over: Home Edition*. It was a spinoff of the original *Extreme Makeover* in which volunteers underwent extensive alterations of their wardrobes, hairstyles, and even bodies (through plastic surgery). Another spinoff was *Extreme Makeover: Weight Loss Edition*. (I'm still hoping for another spinoff: *Extreme Makeover: Church Edition*.)

The makeover shows were popular because all of us are unhappy with something in our lives and would love a quick fix or upgrade. Who wouldn't want a new home or a better wardrobe? Many might even welcome free plastic surgery. In fact, cosmetic surgery is now a huge profit industry in America, with over 15.1 million procedures performed in 2013 (a 100 percent increase in ten years and 750 percent over fifteen years). The use of cosmetic surgery is exploding not only in this country but also in many other nations. People everywhere seem obsessed with changing their bodies.

Why do we humans have such a desire to change our appearances? The answer may surprise you: it is because we long for heaven. Biblically, we all desperately need extreme makeovers (sorry, but it's true).

This reminds me of an Easter choir cantata I once heard about. The

women, singing about their heavenly future, sang, "We shall have new
bodies!" The men responded antiphonally, "Praise the Lord!"

Lord,

>   I confess that I am often unhappy with myself and wish
>   I were taller or thinner or better looking. To be honest,
>   sometimes I make myself miserable hoping my body or
>   face were different.
>   Could it be that this is not my final body? Could this just
>   be the prelude to something more grand and glorious?
>   If it is true that we will all have new bodies in heaven,
>   Christlike bodies that will be youthful and beautiful for-
>   ever, then I too exclaim, Praise the Lord!
>   Amen.

Practical Prayer Pointers

Did your mind wander a bit during the last prayer? If so, why does
this happen more when praying than when talking to a friend? Could
it be that our minds tend to wander more when we pray silently than
when we pray aloud? When we pray silently, it's easy to go off on mental tangents.

I may be praying for a certain friend...which reminds me of another
friend, who happens to be sick...and of another, who just had knee surgery...which reminds me that my knees are beginning to hurt...which
makes me wonder how long I have been praying...because I need to
be done before my lunch appointment...which reminds me that I am
already hungry...which reminds me that I tend to eat too much at
lunches...and thinking about food makes me a bit thirsty...so I reach out
for a drink of water...and notice, next to my water glass, that a new text
has come in on my phone...from the friend that I was praying for...Wait!
Wasn't I just starting to pray for that person? Why did I stop? How did
my mind wander so easily from prayer?

If you can relate with my story, try praying out loud rather than
silently. As long as our mouths are moving and making sounds, it's

harder to wander off topic. It's still possible, but rabbit trails tend to happen when we stop speaking aloud and start thinking silently. It's not that silent prayers are bad; God hears all prayers, whether silent or spoken. It's just that audible prayers keep us better focused.

The Splendor Yet to Come

Long before the television networks orchestrated extreme makeovers, Paul was writing about ultimate, eternal makeovers. In a letter to the church in Corinth, Paul masterfully compared the resurrection to common everyday seeds. When we sow seeds in order to grow plants, the seeds look very different from the mature plant. Who would dream that an acorn would ever become an oak or an egg an ostrich? As Paul put this, each body has its own seed and its own splendor (1 Corinthians 15:35-41). The big surprise is this: we humans are created for incredible splendor, and our earthly bodies are just the seeds. A butterfly has its own beautiful splendor; the caterpillar is just the seed. In the same way, our mature splendor will be realized only in our heavenly bodies.

This is why we are dissatisfied—even downright unhappy—with our earthly bodies.

We put on our cosmetics and toupees, get implants in our breasts and bottoms, and pretend to be what we wish we were. Yes, all of us are vain, which itself is in vain. The cosmetics and surgeries only deny and delay the inevitable. The Bible is honest about this also: "outwardly we are wasting away" (2 Corinthians 4:16a). Our bodies, to put it bluntly, are decaying.

I have heard that our bodies start to die at about age twenty. If you are over that age, have you noticed your step is a bit slower? Is your skin sagging and wrinkling? Is your hair changing colors of its own volition? I remember a conversation with a fellow pastor, quite a celebrity in our circles, whom I learned was my same age. Yet there was not a speck of gray in his dark hair. I asked him about this, and he replied, "I just follow the example of the apostle Paul, who said, 'I dye daily.'"

Solomon did say, "The glory of the young is their strength; the gray hair of experience is the splendor of the old" (Proverbs 20:29 NLT). Yet when I recently looked at a gathering of senior adults, I couldn't help but notice that though the men all had gray hair, the women did not. Apparently, contrary to Solomon, the women did not agree that looking old was a splendid idea. Some men also try to hide the aging process and fight hair decline with strategic hair-combing maneuvers. Maybe we need a new TV show: *Extreme Comb-overs*.

Why do we do all of this? Are we all just insufferably vain, or is there a deeper issue?

What Our Cosmetics Are Covering

Let's stop talking theory and get personal: are you unhappy with something about your body? I know I am. Just a few inches taller and I could reach the top shelves in our home. Just a few pounds lighter and my clothes would fit better. Just a little more hair (okay, a lot more hair) and I could relive the seventies.

So that's my list. What's yours? And why do we all have our lists (even supermodels admit they dislike some aspects of their bodies)?

The answer is that each of us, deep in our soul, longs for something better and different, something *splendid*. But in the seed-like stage, it is quite difficult—maybe even impossible—to imagine what future splendor could look like. Do you think the little caterpillar or larvae could conceive of its extreme makeover?

"Little worm, what you are now is just a seed, but God has created you for much more, for a splendor you can't even begin to imagine. Someday you will feel like you are dying, and out of your apparent death a butterfly will emerge. You will be beautiful beyond imagination. And even better—you will fly."

If a caterpillar could talk, she'd say, "No way. I'm just a caterpillar and never will be beautiful or fly. You are filling my tiny mind with false dreams and hopes."

In the same way, skeptics who are told of life after death say, "No way. I'm just alive for a few years on earth and that's it. You're just talking pie in the sky. I can't conceive of such things as being true."

Oh, but we can and do conceive of such things. We see such extreme makeovers all the time. Acorns to oaks, eggs to birds or reptiles, and, closer to home, sperm and ova into human babies. The seed never begins to express the glory and splendor of its future. As Paul wrote,

> So it will be with the resurrection of the dead. The body that is sown is perishable, it is raised imperishable; it is sown in dishonor, it is raised in glory; it is sown in weakness, it is raised in power; it is sown a natural body, it is raised a spiritual body...
>
> Listen, I tell you a mystery: We will not all sleep, but we will all be changed—in a flash, in the twinkling of an eye, at the last trumpet. For the trumpet will sound, the dead will be raised imperishable, and we will be changed (1 Corinthians 15:42-44,51-52).

There is a beautiful, splendid, eternal being inside you just dying to be born. It's going to happen, and we have proof: Easter was the first eternal, extreme makeover. "Christ has indeed been raised from the dead, the firstfruits of those who have fallen asleep" (1 Corinthians 15:20). A firstfruit is the initial product of the harvest, and it is proof that there is more to come.

Jesus Christ has been raised from the dead, which proves the reality of life after death. The suffering Christ was not the end—the resurrected Christ is the end. And, in a way, it's a preview of our lives to come in heaven. Jesus was resurrected with a perfect, ageless, immortal body, which is what we long for. That's part of what Easter is all about. Here are several stanzas from Charles Wesley's glorious hymn "Christ the Lord Is Risen Today," which captures this truth so well:[2]

> Christ the Lord is risen today, Alleluia!
> Earth and heaven in chorus say, Alleluia!
> Raise your joys and triumphs high, Alleluia!
> Sing, ye heavens, and earth reply, Alleluia!
>
> Love's redeeming work is done, Alleluia!
> Fought the fight, the battle won, Alleluia!
> Death in vain forbids him rise, Alleluia!
> Christ has opened paradise, Alleluia!

Soar we now where Christ has led, Alleluia!
Following our exalted Head, Alleluia!
Made like him, like him we rise, Alleluia!
Ours the cross, the grave, the skies, Alleluia!

Amen and amen!

Jesus' Promises About Heaven

How do we know heaven awaits us, full of infinite wonders, joy, and love? It is because of the many promises Jesus made about our future in heaven.

- "I am the resurrection and the life. Anyone who believes in me will live, even after dying. Everyone who lives in me and believes in me will never ever die" (John 11:25 NLT).

- "Do not let your hearts be troubled. You believe in God; believe also in me. My Father's house has many rooms; if that were not so, would I have told you that I am going there to prepare a place for you? And if I go and prepare a place for you, I will come back and take you to be with me that you also may be where I am" (John 14:1-3).

- "And this is what he has promised us—eternal life" (1 John 2:25).

- "He who testifies to these things says, 'Yes, I am coming soon.' Amen. Come, Lord Jesus. The grace of the Lord Jesus be with God's people. Amen" (Revelation 22:20-21; the last words in the Bible).

This is a veritable smorgasbord of promises, a banquet of blessings. These promises differ, though, from those we have focused on during the previous days of the week. Here Jesus reaches not just into our future lives on earth, but beyond this earth to life eternal. This promise is not just for our mortal todays and tomorrows, it is for our immortal futures when we will enter everlasting life. This promise begins to create and shape our *forevers*. The Bible calls this heaven. It is so glorious that it is also called, not surprisingly, "eternal glory" (1 Peter 5:10).

Until we are called to glory, Jesus promises that he is already there, getting our homes ready for us: "My father's house has many rooms...I am going there to prepare a place for you."[3] How wonderful it will be, after death, when we first arrive to our heavenly homes.

Have you ever traveled to a distant town, bone-weary upon your arrival, and finally reached your hotel? If so, you have probably experienced how wonderful it was to hear the words, "Yes, we have your reservation. Your room is ready." This earthly experience is a little preview of heaven. I believe we will say, "Ah, yes. This is better than I ever imagined, and what I unknowingly have longed for. This is perfect."

Heaven—It's as Real as the Room Next Door

The last book in the Bible begins with, "The revelation from Jesus Christ, which God gave him to show his servants what must soon take place. He made it known by sending his angel to his servant John" (Revelation 1:1). "Must...take place" is a very important phrase, because it shows us that God has future plans that are, in a sense, already real and certain.

The future is as real to God as the next room is to us. God's plans are going to happen, and it's our choice whether we want to be on God's winning side or not. And once we join God's team, we are triumphant even if the scoreboard may now appear to say that we are losing (2 Corinthians 2:14). We have confidence in Christ that no matter how difficult things seem right now, it all makes sense only in light of God's eternal plan.

When our daughter Micah was very young, she repeatedly experienced terrible throat infections until her doctor finally recommended that her tonsils be removed. On the day of the surgery, we knew she would worry if we told her what was happening. So we only said she had a doctor visit, which was the truth (this is a weak attempt to defend my integrity). But as the surgeon did the pre-op examination, Micah realized they were preparing to do an operation. She said, "No—I don't want an operation!" We said, "Honey, you won't be sick so often." She said, "No." We said, "Yes." Finally, with tears running down her checks, she said to me, "Daddy, don't let them do this to me!" I wanted to cave and give in to her, but I didn't—because I could see the long-term plan. But she couldn't see it, so she was understandably panicked.

It's the same with us and God. We can't see his long-term plan. Here's Randy Alcorn's helpful way to illustrate this reality:[4]

Time on Earth   Time in Heaven

Our whole lives on earth are like a dot compared to eternity in heaven. Our lives may seem long now, but they will shrink in size and importance when we see the heavenly perspective. If we can grasp that God has an eternal plan for us, then we can handle the problems during our miniscule (in comparison) earthly sojourn.

What Will Heaven Be Like? And What Will We Be Like in Heaven?

Let's take the second question first. Paul wrote, "Just as we have borne the image of the earthly man, so shall we bear the image of the heavenly man" (1 Corinthians 15:49). In other words, we will be like Jesus in heaven. Our natural bodies were made for earth, but our resurrection bodies will be made for heaven.

Furthermore, after Jesus' resurrection appearances and before the ascension, we were given a quick view of Jesus' heavenly body. Since we will be like him, this is therefore also a glimpse of our own future resurrection bodies. This is a fascinating topic for further study, so here is a quick overview of some of the key qualities of Jesus' resurrection body, which also may describe our future heavenly bodies:

- He was identifiable (Mark 16:12).
- He was relational (John 21:15-17).
- He was touchable (Luke 24:39).
- He was not spatially limited (John 20:19; Luke 24:36).
- He could rise into the air (Luke 24:51).
- He fished and ate (John 21:9; Luke 24:42-43).
- He entered paradise (Luke 23:43).

Now to the first question, "What will heaven be like?" The short answer is, we have so much to look forward to in heaven—joy and love and peace beyond imagination—but now can only faintly perceive it, as "in a mirror dimly" (1 Corinthians 13:12 NASB). A full discussion of these pleasures is beyond the scope of this book,[5] but at least we know that "there will be no more death or mourning or crying or pain, for the old order of things has passed away" (Revelation 21:4).

May it suffice to say that we are dissatisfied here on earth because we long for eternity and immortality. God "has also set eternity in the human heart" (Ecclesiastes 3:11), and we deeply intuit that we should not die. Death is an enemy to be defeated, not yielded to. This is why even atheists try to live as long as they can. Their spirits rebel against mortality, even as their minds try to deny their supernatural and eternal intuitions.

Nonetheless, they try to prolong their lives and pretty up their dying bodies, which is as ineffective as stapling wings on caterpillars or gluing acorns together to form an oak tree. It will never work because "flesh and blood cannot inherit the kingdom of God, nor does the perishable inherit the imperishable" (1 Corinthians 15:50).

Jesus also has promised that, when the time is right, he will return for us, defeat the evil enemy, and take his followers to heaven. This was the hope of the early church, expressed in the Aramaic phrase, *Maranatha*, which means "Come, Lord!" (1 Corinthians 16:22). And it is with this promise that the whole Bible ends, "Yes, I am coming soon" (Revelation 22:20-21).

What Happens After We Die?

The most important thing to know about death is that it's not the end. This is why Paul wrote, "We will not all sleep, but we will all be changed" (1 Corinthians 15:51). When the number of our allotted days comes to an end (Psalm 39:4), each human being will stand before God's judgment throne, as the writer of Hebrews says, "Just as people are destined to die once, and after that to face judgment, so Christ was sacrificed once to take away the sins of many; and he will appear a second time, not to bear sin, but to bring salvation to those who are waiting for him" (9:27-28). For each of us, this appointment already has been scheduled.

When we die, we don't cease to live. All of us will continue to exist, Christians and non-Christians, believers and nonbelievers, theists and nontheists. And we all will undergo ultimate, extreme makeovers. Since the resurrected body of Jesus was the first and ultimate Extreme Makeover, Christians also will get new bodies like his. "We know that when Christ appears we shall be like him, for we shall see him as he is" (1 John 3:2b).

But for nonbelievers, it will be a summation of all the ways they have lived contrary to God's will. It will be a makeover gone terribly bad, an extreme mess-over, like Gollum in Tolkien's *Lord of the Rings*. Jesus himself said, "Do not be amazed at this, for a time is coming when all who are in their graves will hear his voice and come out—those who have done what is good will rise to live, and those who have done what is evil will rise to be condemned" (John 5:28). It's a tough truth to swallow, but that's what's going to happen to anyone whose name isn't in the Lamb's book of life (Revelation 20:15).

When will Jesus return? We don't know the exact time, but we know exactly how to spot it. "We will not all sleep, but we will all be changed— in a flash, in the twinkling of an eye, at the last trumpet. For the trumpet will sound, the dead will be raised imperishable, and we will be changed" (1 Corinthians 15:51-52). The last trumpet refers to the Second Coming, the glorious return of Jesus (Matthew 24:30-31).

On **S**aturdays, we remind ourselves to constantly listen for that sound, to be ever ready for his return. We pray, "I'm **S**o excited about heaven!"

When Jesus returns, it will be Easter—forever.

We will be together with saved loved ones—forever.

We will have new perfect bodies—forever.

We will be forgiven and pure, never to sin again—forever.

We will be protected from evil—forever.

We will never experience pain or suffering—forever.

We will be in paradise—forever.

It's not fantasy or make-believe; it is true and it "must happen."

We have been promised that it will be glorious, splendid, and magnificent.

It sounds like...like heaven.

Lord,

Today we look forward to your glorious appearance. As
when we worship with bread and wine, we proclaim
your death until you come. You said, "I am the Alpha
and the Omega, who is, and who was, and who is to
come." We know that you are not slow in keeping your
promise, but patient, not wanting anyone to perish, but
everyone to come to repentance.

And we know that all of creation now groans in frustration,
awaiting your return, longing to be liberated from its
bondage to decay. We know that when you come, like
a thief in the night, the heavens will disappear with a
roar, the elements will be destroyed by fire, and the earth
and everything done in it will be laid bare. Then a new
heaven and earth will be created, for the first heaven and
the first earth will have passed away.

Holy, holy, holy, is the Lord God Almighty, who was, and
is, and is to come. You have said, "Yes, I am coming
soon."

Amen. Come, Lord Jesus.

PART THREE

A One-Month Adventure in
Praying the Promises of Jesus

11

Instructions for Using the
Daily Prayer Guides

*"For no matter how many promises God
has made, they are 'Yes' in Christ."*

2 Corinthians 1:20

In part 3 of this book, I invite you on a one-month prayer adventure. We will pray together through four weeks of daily prayer guides, which will help us learn the *Praying the Promises of Jesus* method. Each day follows a simple pattern:

- First, we begin by recording the date and the names of those for whom we are praying.

- Second, we will prayerfully offer up to God at least two Scriptures, which are provided to ground our prayer time in God's Word and in that day's theme.

- Third, a Daily Prayer Opener helps remind us of the power of Jesus' promises to shape our future, and how great and precious are his promises to believers.

- Fourth, a Promise Prayer guides us through each day's promises and provides numerous additional Scriptures to pray.

As you will see, these prayers are thoroughly based upon and infused with Scripture. As we follow this guide, we pray God's Word back to him, as a child repeats her parents' words in order to learn language. We speak the language of God, using his own vocabulary and syntax as much as possible. Over time, we will find ourselves effortlessly memorizing many passages and phrases from Scripture. As the psalmist prayed, "I have hidden your word in my heart" (Psalm 119:11), we will find that praying the promises of Jesus slowly fills our minds and souls with his Word, wisdom, and confidence.

Daily Prayer Scriptures

As we begin to pray each day, it helps center our souls to read and pray Scripture. This is why each day's prayer guide begins with two Scriptures: the key promise of Jesus for that day of the week and a supportive Scripture to reinforce the day's central promise.

It is my prayer that, in time, you will naturally associate each day of the week with both the day's theme and its key promise (see appendix). For instance, on Sundays you will pray, all day long, "I'm Surrounded by his love, because Jesus promised to be with me always, even to the end of the age."

Each day's theme and Scriptures complement one another and are meant to be prayed rather than merely read. On Thursday of week two, for example, the two Scriptures appear like this:

Scriptures
Thursday's key promise from Jesus:

> "Come to me, all you who are weary and burdened, and I will give you rest" (Matthew 11:28).

Supportive promise from Scripture:

> "Cast all your anxiety on him because he cares for you" (1 Peter 5:7).

I suggest that you read these verses as prayers, such as, "Lord, you have promised in your Word, saying, 'Come to me, all you who are weary and burdened, and I will give you rest.' And the Bible also says, 'Cast all your anxiety on him because he cares for you.' Thank you for these very great and precious promises."

Daily Prayer Openers

In my own prayer life I find it very helpful, after focusing my mind through praying Scriptures, to pray a Daily Prayer Opener. This is a short summary of the power of promises and how Jesus shapes our lives through them. It is also a confession of why we need to pray and an appeal for God's help in becoming the persons God created us to be.

I recommend that you pray this prayer, aloud and word for word, each day for the first week of our prayer journey. To help you with this, this prayer will be repeated the first three days during the first week. Thereafter, you will be reminded to pray the Daily Prayer Opener, but it will not be reprinted each day. I recommend that you write the prayer on a bookmark or sticky note, which allows you to move it from page to page, one day at a time. Or you can memorize the prayer from the get-go. But don't get rigid; feel free to allow the Daily Prayer Opener to morph and match your personality and style.

In time, you will find that you have naturally memorized the essential parts of *Praying the Promises of Jesus*, and you will be able to pray according to this method even when this book is not at hand. You may be riding on a bus, driving in your car, or even interacting with someone who, it occurs to you, is in need of the encouragement of a certain promise. For instance, maybe a friend complains about loneliness, and you feel called to pray for him. Before you pray for him, though, you feel drawn to pray first for yourself, for humility as you deal with this lonely person and as you confess to God that you have often felt lonely also. Thank Jesus for his promise to always be with you even until the end of the age and ask him to help you to feel his presence strongly today. Then pray a similar prayer for your friend.

Here is the Daily Prayer Opener that we can pray for ourselves:

Dear Lord,

> I believe that your promises are great and precious and
> have the power to tremendously improve my life. So I
> ask you to shape my life through your promises; mold
> my plans, my relationships, and my destiny. I pray that
> your promises, Jesus, would gain control of my beliefs,
> thoughts, and behaviors so that my life might become
> what you intended it to be.

I also thank you for the tremendous power you have

given me to reach out into tomorrow and create a better future through making and keeping promises of my
own. I want to be a faithful person whose word is trustworthy, for your Word promises that you will not forsake your faithful ones. So I ask you, dear Jesus, to give
me the strength to be like you: a wise promise-maker
and faithful promise-keeper.
In your name I pray. Amen.

I suggest that you use this simple prayer, or something like it, to
begin your daily time of praying the promises of Jesus. I enjoy praying
some form of this introductory prayer for myself, each day, to focus my
heart and mind. I also enjoy praying some variation of this prayer for
those on my prayer list. For instance, I may pray for my daughter:

Dear Lord,

I believe that your promises are great and precious and
have the power to tremendously improve Micah's life.
So I ask you to shape her life through your promises;
mold her plans, her relationships, and her destiny. I pray
that your promises, Jesus, would gain control of her
beliefs, thoughts, and behaviors so that her life might
become what you intended it to be.
I also thank you for the tremendous power you have given
Micah to reach out into tomorrow and create a better future through making and keeping promises of her
own. I ask you to help Micah become a faithful person whose word is trustworthy, for your Word promises
that you will not forsake your faithful ones. So I ask you,
dear Jesus, to give her the strength to be like you: a wise
promise-maker and faithful promise-keeper.
In your name I pray. Amen.

With this in mind, let's proceed to Week One of the prayer guides for
Praying the Promises of Jesus.

12

WEEK ONE
Starting to Pray the Promises of Jesus

"For no matter how many promises God has made, they are 'Yes' in Christ."

2 CORINTHIANS 1:20

Instructions for Week One

This week we will learn how to pray the promises of Jesus for ourselves. At first this may seem a bit self-centered to begin by praying for ourselves, but it is best to learn to pray for ourselves before we venture on to pray for others.

Most of us have experienced what may be a helpful analogy: during the preflight instructions given to airline passengers before takeoff, parents are instructed to put on their own oxygen masks before they help their children with their masks. This order is helpful in the Christian life generally: it is best to take the log out of one's own eye before trying to help someone else with a splinter (Matthew 7:5). The same is true with prayer. I have always found that I can better pray for others after I first have dealt personally and honestly with the Lord.

In addition, praying the promises of Jesus into our own lives is a good first-week topic because it is not complex or difficult. We easily can begin to learn the flow of praying in this manner. In the weeks that follow, we will introduce new prayers with varying degrees of complexity.

Let's begin by recording today's date and praying the following Scriptures and prayers aloud.

SUNDAY: I'm Surrounded by Love

Lord, today I enter your presence and pray for myself:

Date: _____

(Use the following spaces for future weeks when you cycle again through these prayers.)

Date: _____ Date: _____ Date: _____ Date: _____

Date: _____ Date: _____ Date: _____ Date: _____

Scriptures

Sunday's key promise from Jesus:

> "Surely I am with you always, to the very end of the age"
> (Matthew 28:20).

Supportive promise from Scripture:

> "Never will I leave you;
> never will I forsake you."
>   (Hebrews 13:5)

Daily Prayer Opener

Dear Lord,

I believe that your promises are great and precious and have the power to tremendously improve my life. So I ask you to shape my life through your promises; mold my plans, my relationships, and my destiny. I pray that your promises, Jesus, would gain control of my beliefs, thoughts, and behaviors so that my life might become what you intended it to be.

I also thank you for the tremendous power you have given me to reach out into tomorrow and create a better future through making and keeping promises of my own. I want to be a faithful person whose word is trustworthy, for your Word promises that you will not forsake your faithful ones. So I ask you, dear Jesus, to give me the strength to be like you: a wise promise-maker and faithful promise-keeper.

In your name I pray. Amen.

Promise Prayer

Lord:

It's Sunday, so I'm Surrounded by your love today. Please remind me that I'm no longer alone. It is so good to know that you planned, long ago, to be with me today. Lord, that's an appointment I want to keep. Even when I struggle with loneliness or heartache, you have said you will never leave me or forsake me, and I hold tight to that promise in my life.

I pray that you would help me to feel your love today and that I would be able to share that love with others. When I feel alone, I know that you always are with me. I pray that my love for you would be made complete and that I would know that perfect love drives out all fear. Today, I will not be afraid, for you are with me, and your rod and staff comfort me.

Lord, you love me so much you gave your life for me. Please help me to always remember that nothing can separate me from your love and that unfailing love surrounds the one who trusts in you.

In your loving name, I pray. Amen.

> Hebrews 13:5; John 15:12-13; 1 John 4:7; Deuteronomy 31:6; 1 John 2:5; 4:18; Psalm 118:6; 23:4; John 3:16; Romans 8:38-39; Psalm 32:10

MONDAY: I'm Making Happiness a Habit

Lord, today I enter your presence and pray for myself:

Date: _____ Date: _____ Date: _____ Date: _____

Date: _____ Date: _____ Date: _____ Date: _____

Scriptures

Monday's key promise from Jesus:

> "I have told you this so that my joy may be in you and that your joy may be complete" (John 15:11).

Supportive promise from Scripture:

> "You make known to me the path of life;
>   you will fill me with joy in your presence,
>   with eternal pleasures at your right hand."
>   (Psalm 16:11)

Daily Prayer Opener

Dear Lord,

I believe that your promises are great and precious and have the power to tremendously improve my life. So I ask you to shape my life through your promises; mold my plans, my relationships, and my destiny. I pray that your promises, Jesus, would gain control of my beliefs, thoughts, and behaviors so that my life might become what you intended it to be.

I also thank you for the tremendous power you have given me to reach out into tomorrow and create a better future through making and keeping promises of my own. I want to be a faithful person whose word is trustworthy, for your Word promises that you will not forsake your faithful ones. So I ask you, dear

Jesus, to give me the strength to be like you: a wise promise-maker and faithful promise-keeper.

In your name I pray. Amen.

Promise Prayer

Lord,

It's Monday, so I'm Making happiness a habit today. You reached into the future long ago and promised to give me your joy; that's a promise I hope to receive from you today. I pray that you would help me to shout for joy to the Lord, for great is the Holy One among us. Help me to be filled with your joy as I wake up, as I go about my day, as I come home, and as I fall asleep. Help me be joyful always, because you are with me.

I pray that I would consider it pure joy whenever I face trials of many kinds, because the testing of my faith produces perseverance. I pray that today I would find joy even when the future is uncertain. I pray that you would make known to me the path of life. Help me understand that in your presence there is fullness of joy and at your right hand there are pleasures forevermore. Lord, I put my trust in you.

In your joyful name, I pray. Amen.

Psalm 100:1; Isaiah 12:6; 1 Thessalonians 5:16; Romans 14:17;
1 Thessalonians 2:20; James 1:2-3; Psalm 16:11; 86:4

TUESDAY: I'm Trusting in God's Strength

Lord, today I enter your presence and pray for myself:

Date: _____ Date: _____ Date: _____ Date: _____

Date: _____ Date: _____ Date: _____ Date: _____

Scriptures

Tuesday's key promise from Jesus:

> "Truly I tell you, if you have faith as small as a mustard seed, you can say to this mountain, 'Move from here to there,' and it will move. Nothing will be impossible for you" (Matthew 17:20-21).

Supportive promise from Scripture:

> "He gives strength to the weary
> and increases the power of the weak."
> (Isaiah 40:29)

Daily Prayer Opener

Dear Lord,

I believe that your promises are great and precious and have the power to tremendously improve my life. So I ask you to shape my life through your promises; mold my plans, my relationships, and my destiny. I pray that your promises, Jesus, would gain control of my beliefs, thoughts, and behaviors so that my life might become what you intended it to be.

I also thank you for the tremendous power you have given me to reach out into tomorrow and create a better future through making and keeping promises of my own. I want to be a faithful person whose word is trustworthy, for your Word promises that you will not forsake your faithful ones. So I ask you, dear Jesus, to give me the strength to be like you: a wise promise-maker and faithful promise-keeper.

In your name I pray. Amen.

Promise Prayer

Lord,

It's Tuesday, so I'm Trusting in your strength today. I pray that when my strength is weak and my hope is fading, I will remember that you are my refuge and strength, an ever-present help in trouble, and that your power is made perfect in weakness. I pray that you will help me to know that you work all things for the good of those who love you, who have been called according to your purpose.

When I ask, with Job, "What strength do I have, that I should still hope? What prospects, that I should be patient?" I pray that, like Job, I will learn that you can do all things, and no plan of yours can be thwarted. I choose to trust in you today, tomorrow, and in the future. Help me to be still before you, wait patiently for you, and believe that I can do all things because you give me strength.

Lord, I pray for the strength to trust in you with all my heart and lean not on my own understanding. Help me in all my ways to submit to you, for you have promised to make my paths straight.

In your powerful name. Amen.

> Psalm 46:1; 2 Corinthians 12:9; Romans 8:28; Job 6:11; 42:1-2; Psalm 37:7; Philippians 4:13; Psalm 31:24; Proverbs 3:5-6

WEDNESDAY: I'm Wanting What God Wants

Lord, today I enter your presence and pray for myself:

Date: _____ Date: _____ Date: _____ Date: _____

Date: _____ Date: _____ Date: _____ Date: _____

Scriptures

Wednesday's key promise from Jesus:

> "You may ask me for anything in my name, and I will do it" (John 14:14).

Supportive promise from Scripture:

> "I desire to do your will, my God;
> your law is within my heart."
> (Psalm 40:8)

Daily Prayer Opener

(See page 124)

Promise Prayer

Lord,

It's Wednesday, so today I'm Wanting what you want. I ask for your will to become my will, Lord. I pray that with all of the temptations facing me each day that I will not be conformed to the pattern of this world, but be transformed by the renewing of my mind so that I can discern your good, pleasing, and perfect will.

I pray that when I am uncertain about what to do, where I am to go, and what decisions to make, that I will learn to say, "If it is the Lord's will, I will live and do this or that." I pray that you would help me to know what is good and what you require of me, which is to act justly and to love mercy and to walk humbly with you, God. I pray that I may live a life worthy of you, Lord, and may please you in every way, bearing fruit in every good work.

Lord, I seek not my own will but the will of "him who sent me." Help me to not be foolish but to understand what your will is. I ask for you to help me trust the plans you have for me, plans to prosper me and not to harm me, plans to give me hope and a future. I seek you, Lord, with all my heart, and I surrender myself completely to your will.

According to your will, Lord Jesus, I pray. Amen.

Romans 12:2; James 4:15; Colossians 1:10; John 5:30; Ephesians 5:17; Jeremiah 29:11,13

THURSDAY: I'm Trading My Troubles for Peace

Lord, today I enter your presence and pray for myself:

Date: _____ Date: _____ Date: _____ Date: _____

Date: _____ Date: _____ Date: _____ Date: _____

Scriptures

Thursday's key promise from Jesus:

> "Come to me, all you who are weary and burdened, and I will give you rest" (Matthew 11:28).

Supportive promise from Scripture:

> "Peace I leave with you; my peace I give you. I do not give to you as the world gives. Do not let your hearts be troubled and do not be afraid" (John 14:27).

Daily Prayer Opener

(See page 124)

Promise Prayer

Lord,

It's Thursday, so I'm Trading my troubles for peace today. Help me to not be anxious about anything, or worry about what tomorrow will hold. Instead, help me realize that you know what I need before I ask, and peace comes from trusting you to provide, as I seek first your kingdom and righteousness.

Lord, peace seems to elude me and fear takes hold of my heart. Please deliver me from all my fears, for I know you can calm the storm to a whisper and bring stillness through your unfailing love. Lord, I ask you to help me to find moments where I can find rest for my soul, and remind me I can soar on wings like eagles, run and not grow weary, and walk and not be faint.

Help me today to set my heart and mind on things above, not on earthly things. May the peace of Christ rule in my heart, and may I be thankful for the life you have given me. I ask you to fill me today with your peace that transcends all understanding, which will guard my heart and mind in Christ Jesus.

In your peaceful name, I pray. Amen.

> Philippians 4:6; Matthew 6:25,32-34; Psalm 107:29-31; Matthew 11:29; Isaiah 40:31; Colossians 3:1-2,15; Philippians 4:7

FRIDAY: I'm Finding Freedom

Lord, today I enter your presence and pray for myself:

Date: _____ Date: _____ Date: _____ Date: _____

Date: _____ Date: _____ Date: _____ Date: _____

Scriptures

Friday's key promise from Jesus:

> "If the Son sets you free, you will be free indeed" (John 8:36).

Supportive promise from Scripture:

> "Be kind and compassionate to one another, forgiving each other, just as in Christ God forgave you" (Ephesians 4:32).

Daily Prayer Opener

(See page 124)

Promise Prayer

Lord,

It's Friday, so I'm Finding freedom today. Lord, please help me to fully understand the impact of your sacrifice. Because of the cross, I'm free—completely free.

Lord, you have told us that if we confess our sins, you are faithful and just to forgive us. Help me forgive others as you have forgiven me. I pray that my heart will be free to trust in you. Your Word says that we are called to be free and are not to use our freedom to indulge the sinful nature. Instead, we are to serve one another in love, so I pray that in my freedom I will reach out in love and serve wholeheartedly.

Lord, where the Spirit of the Lord is, there is freedom, so I pray that I will reflect your glory and be transformed into your likeness as I follow you, in freedom, all the days of my life.

In your freeing name, I pray. Amen.

> Ephesians 1:7; 1 John 1:9; John 8:11; Romans 3:23; Colossians 3:13; Galatians 5:13; 2 Corinthians 3:18

SATURDAY: I'm So Excited About Heaven

Lord, today I enter your presence and pray for myself:

Date: _____ Date: _____ Date: _____ Date: _____

Date: _____ Date: _____ Date: _____ Date: _____

Scriptures

Saturday's key promise from Jesus:

> "In My Father's house are many dwelling places; if it were not so, I would have told you; for I go to prepare a place for you" (John 14:2 NASB).

Supportive promise from Scripture:

> "He will wipe every tear from their eyes. There will be no more death or mourning or crying or pain, for the old order of things has passed away" (Revelation 21:4).

Daily Prayer Opener

(See page 124)

Promise Prayer

Lord,

It's Saturday, and I'm So excited about heaven.

I can't wait until I walk through the heavenly gates and hear these words, "Well done, good and faithful servant. You have been faithful with a few things; I will put you in charge of many things. Come and share your master's happiness." Lord, sometimes life is difficult and the burdens are so heavy that I groan, longing to be clothed with my heavenly dwelling. I live each day by faith and not by sight, and I long to be at home with you, Lord.

You have said, "I am coming soon," so I eagerly wait for the day you will come down from heaven with a loud command and trumpet call, and we will rise up in the clouds to meet you in the air. What a glorious day that will be. Until that time, I pray today that I can live a life, here on earth, worthy of the calling I have received, and no longer live as one tossed back and forth by the waves and blown here and there by every storm.

Lord, help me to keep my eyes focused on heaven today and ready myself for the mansion you have prepared for me in heaven.

In your heavenly name, I pray. Amen.

> Matthew 25:21; 2 Corinthians 5:2,7-8; Revelation 22:12; 1 Thessalonians 4:16-17; Romans 2:6; Matthew 16:24; Ephesians 4:1, 14; John 14:2

13

WEEK TWO

Praying the Promises
of Jesus for Others

*"For no matter how many promises God
has made, they are 'Yes' in Christ."*

2 Corinthians 1:20

Instructions for Week Two

In Week Two we want to begin to pray for our families. Now that we've taken the time to pray for ourselves, we can easily adapt our prayer method to include our spouses, children, parents, close friends, brothers, and sisters—everyone we consider our important friends and family. We can tremendously help them by praying the promises of Jesus into their lives. In many cases, unless we do this, they may never have anyone praying these themes for them.

SUNDAY: I'm Surrounded by Love

Lord, today I lift up prayer for:

Date: _____ Names: _____

(Use the following space for future weeks when you cycle again through these prayers.)

Date: _____ Names: _____

Date: _____ Names: _____

Date: _____ Names: _____

Date: _____ Names: _____

Scriptures

Sunday's key promise from Jesus:

> "Surely I am with you always, to the very end of the age"
> (Matthew 28:20).

Supportive promise from Scripture:

> "No one will be able to stand against you all the days of
> your life. As I was with Moses, so I will be with you; I will
> never leave you nor forsake you" (Joshua 1:5).

Daily Prayer Opener

(See page 124)

Promise Prayer

Lord,

It's Sunday, so I pray for these important people in my life
_____ (insert names here) to be Surrounded by love
and no longer feel alone today. I pray that just as you were
with Moses, so you will be with _____ today and help
them to know you will never leave nor forsake them.

Help _____ see what great love you have lavished on
them, that they should be called children of God. You have
summoned them by name, and they are yours. Even when
they pass through the waters and walk through fire, you will
be with them. I pray you would help them when discouraged

to know that you are near to all who call on you and that you
hear their cry and will comfort them.

Lord, I pray that you would help my loved ones know that you
watch over all who love you. No matter what today holds for
them, draw them close and surround them with your love.
Help them to know you are with them, that you take great
delight in them, and that you will quiet them with your love
and rejoice over them with singing.

In Jesus' loving name. Amen.

> Joshua 1:5; 1 John 3:1a; Psalm 25:16; Matthew 28:20; Isaiah
> 43:1-5; Psalm 145:18-20a; Zephaniah 3:17

MONDAY: I'm Making Happiness a Habit

Lord, today I lift up prayer for:

Date: _____ Names: _____

(Use the following space for future weeks when you cycle again through
these prayers.)

Date: _____ Names: _____

Date: _____ Names: _____

Date: _____ Names: _____

Date: _____ Names: _____

Scriptures

Monday's key promise from Jesus:

> "I have told you this so that my joy may be in you and that
> your joy may be complete" (John 15:11).

Supportive promise or Scripture:

> "Very truly I tell you, you will weep and mourn while the
> world rejoices. You will grieve, but your grief will turn to
> joy" (John 16:20).

Daily Prayer Opener
(See page 124)

Promise Prayer
Lord,

It's Monday, so today I pray for my family and friends,
_____, to make happiness a habit. I pray that you,
the God of hope, will fill them with all joy and peace as they
trust in you so that they may overflow with hope by the power
of the Holy Spirit.

May this be a day in which their hearts are glad, their tongues
rejoice, and their bodies rest secure, because with you at their
right hand they will not be shaken. Lord, life has its times of
sadness and sorrow, so I pray today that you would help them
know that those who sow in tears shall reap with songs of joy
and those who go out weeping will return with songs of praise.

May your joy, O Lord, be their strength today. May you make
known to them the paths of life, and may you fill them with
gladness in your presence. I pray you would fill their mouth
with laughter and their lips with shouts of joy.

In Jesus' blessed name. Amen.

> Romans 15:13; Psalm 16:8-9; 126:5-6; Nehemiah 8:10; Acts
> 2:28; Job 8:21

TUESDAY: I'm Trusting in God's Strength

Lord, today I lift up prayer for:

Date: _____ Names: _____

(Use the following space for future weeks when you cycle again through these prayers.)

Date: _____ Names: _____

Date: _____ Names: _____

Date: _____ Names: _____

Date: _____ Names: _____

Scriptures

Tuesday's key promise from Jesus:

> "Truly I tell you, if you have faith as small as a mustard seed, you can say to this mountain, 'Move from here to there,' and it will move. Nothing will be impossible for you" (Matthew 17:20-21).

Supportive promise from Scripture:

> "So do not fear, for I am with you;
>   do not be dismayed, for I am your God.
> I will strengthen you and help you;
>   I will uphold you with my righteous right hand."
>   (Isaiah 41:10)

Daily Prayer Opener

(See page 124)

Promise Prayer

Lord,

It's Tuesday, so today I pray for my family and friends to trust in your strength. I pray for those who are feeling overwhelmed with responsibilities at home and work. Please help them know that with your power that is at work in them, you can help them to do immeasurably more than all they can ask or imagine.

I pray for _____ to learn to be patient, as you are patient with us. As the farmer waits for the land to yield its valuable crop and patiently waits for the autumn and spring rains, help my loved ones to know that they too can be patient and stand firm.

Help them to not grow weary of doing good in their daily lives and to remember that they will reap a harvest if they do not give up. May their faith not rest on human wisdom but on your power and insight, for no eye has seen, no ear heard, and no mind has conceived what you have prepared for those who love you.

May they know that nothing is impossible with you, Lord. May the eyes of their heart be enlightened in order that they may know the hope to which you have called them and experience your incomparably great power given to those who believe.

In Jesus' strong name I pray. Amen.

> Ephesians 3:20; Psalm 130:5; 102:1-2; Colossians 1:11; James 5:7-8; Galatians 6:9; 1 Corinthians 2:5,9; Luke 1:37; Ephesians 1:18-19

WEDNESDAY: I'm Wanting What God Wants

Lord, today I lift up prayer for:

Date: _____ Names: _____

(Use the following space for future weeks when you cycle again through these prayers.)

Date: _____ Names: _____

Date: _____ Names: _____

Date: _____ Names: _____

Date: _____ Names: _____

Scriptures

Wednesday's key promise from Jesus:

> "You may ask me for anything in my name, and I will do it" (John 14:14).

Supportive promise from Scripture:

> "Your kingdom come, your will be done on earth as it is in heaven" (Matthew 6:10).

Daily Prayer Opener

(See page 124)

Promise Prayer

Lord,

It's Wednesday, so I pray for my family and friends to learn to want what you want, for your will to be their will, Lord. I pray they would learn that seeking their own desires leads to disappointment, whereas delighting themselves in you leads to receiving the desires of their heart.

I pray for _____ who are lost in their own cravings, the lust of their eyes, and the boasting of what they have done, to see that those desires will pass away, but the ones who do your will, Lord, live forever.

Lord, please help _____ who is battling self-doubt and lack of confidence. Help them know that they are your workmanship, created in Christ Jesus to do good works, which you prepared in advance for them to do. You formed them in the womb and set them apart before they were born.

I pray that they will give thanks in all circumstances, for this is your will for them in Christ Jesus. I pray that, as they go about their business, school, or whatever they do, that they would do it with all their hearts, working for you, Lord, and not for themselves.

In Jesus' name I pray. Amen.

> Psalm 37:4; 1 John 2:16-17; Psalm 32:8-9; Ephesians 2:10; Jeremiah 1:5; 1 Thessalonians 5:18; Colossians 3:23-24

THURSDAY: I'm Trading My Troubles for Peace

Lord, today I lift up prayer for:

Date: _____ Names: _____

(Use the following space for future weeks when you cycle again through these prayers.)

Date: _____ Names: _____

Date: _____ Names: _____

Date: _____ Names: _____

Date: _____ Names: _____

Scriptures

Thursday's key promise from Jesus:

> "Come to me, all you who are weary and burdened, and I
> will give you rest" (Matthew 11:28).

Supportive promise from Scripture:

> "Cast all your anxiety on him because he cares for you"
> (1 Peter 5:7).

Daily Prayer Opener

(See page 124)

Promise Prayer

Lord,

It's Thursday, so I pray that my loved ones can trade their troubles for peace.

Lord, I pray for those who are worried today about many things—finances, job security, relationships, or health, just to mention a few. They are drowning under the pressures of these worries. I pray that they will know they can ask and it will be given to them, seek and they will find, and knock and the doors will be opened to them, for you know what we need even before we ask.

My prayers are lifted for _____, that you would be a shield around them, O Lord. Bestow glory on them and lift up their heads. I pray that you would help them to be strong and courageous, not terrified or discouraged, for you are with them.

I pray that my family and friends would make every effort to live in peace with each other and to be holy, so that no bitter root grows up to cause trouble. I pray that your love would increase in them for each other so that they will be pleasing in your sight and pleasant to be around when together.

In Jesus' fearless name I pray. Amen.

> Matthew 7:7-8; Isaiah 26:3; Psalm 3:3; Joshua 1:9; John 16:33; Hebrews 12:14-15; 1 Thessalonians 3:12-13

FRIDAY: I'm Finding Freedom

Lord, today I lift up prayer for:

Date: _____ Names: _____

(Use the following space for future weeks when you cycle again through these prayers.)

Date: _____ Names: _____

Date: _____ Names: _____

Date: _____ Names: _____

Date: _____ Names: _____

Scriptures

Friday's key promise from Jesus:

> "If the Son sets you free, you will be free indeed" (John 8:36).

Supportive promise from Scripture:

> "Without the shedding of blood there is no forgiveness" (Hebrews 9:22b).

Daily Prayer Opener

(See page 124)

Promise Prayer

Lord:

It's Friday, so today I pray that my friends and family would find true freedom in their lives. I pray especially for those who do not know you and who are enslaved to sin. I pray they would come to repent of their sins, place their faith in you alone, and become new creations.

Lord, I thank you for giving my family the freedom to choose whom we will serve, and I pray with Joshua, "As for me and my household, we will serve the Lord." May my family continue to choose you from generation to generation, and be a chosen community called out of darkness into the marvelous light.

Lord, I pray for _____who are weighed down under the burden of the past. I pray that you could loose the chains of injustice and set them free. Since such a great cloud of witnesses surrounds them, let them throw off everything that hinders and the sin that so easily entangles, and let them run with perseverance the race marked out for them. May they fix their eyes on you, Jesus, and truly be set free.

In your perfect name, I pray. Amen.

> 2 Corinthians 5:17; Romans 6:18; Joshua 24:14-15; 1 Peter 2:9;
> Matthew 5:44; 5:39; Isaiah 58:6; Hebrews 12:1-2

SATURDAY: I'm So Excited About Heaven

Lord, today I lift up prayer for:

Date: _____ Names: _____

(Use the following space for future weeks when you cycle again through these prayers.)

Date: _____ Names: _____

Date: _____ Names: _____

Date: _____ Names: _____

Date: _____ Names: _____

Scriptures

Saturday's key promise from Jesus:

> "In My Father's house are many dwelling places; if it were
> not so, I would have told you; for I go to prepare a place
> for you" (John 14:2 NASB).

Supportive promise from Scripture:

> "'What no eye has seen,
>   what no ear has heard,
> and what no human mind has conceived'—
>   the things God has prepared for those who love him—
> these are the things God has revealed to us by his Spirit."
>   (1 Corinthians 2:9-10)

Daily Prayer Opener

(See page 124)

Promise Prayer

Lord,

It's Saturday, so today I pray for my family and friends to be
excited about heaven. Lord, I pray that they would be encouraged each day to look forward to your glorious appearing. For
their citizenship is in heaven where you will bring everything
under your control and transform their lowly bodies to be like
your glorious body.

Help them to remember that they should not store up for themselves treasures on earth, where moth and rust destroy, and where thieves break in and steal. Instead, remind them to store up for themselves treasures in heaven, for where their treasure is, their hearts will be also.

I pray also for _____, who are not saved and do not know you, Lord. They have no idea of the blessings or beauty of living with you forever in heaven. May they come to know that you died for their sins and that repentant believers in Jesus will be saved. Convince them of the importance of assuring that their names are written in the Lamb's book of life, so they will live in heaven—forever.

In your awesome name, I pray. Amen.

> Titus 2:13; Philippians 3:20-21; Acts 1:7-8,11; 1 Peter 5:8-10; Ephesians 2:6; Matthew 6:19-20; Revelation 21:3; Romans 6:23; 1 Peter 3:18; Acts 16:31; Revelation 20:15

14

WEEK THREE
Praying the Promises of Jesus as Reflected in the Old Testament

"Not one of all the LORD's good promises to Israel failed; every one was fulfilled."

JOSHUA 21:45

As we pray the promises of Jesus in Week Three, we do so in light of the backdrop of the Old Testament. God's promises, given and kept in the centuries before Jesus came to earth, were recorded there. The promises of Jesus did not suddenly appear but were foretold and anticipated over thousands of years. In a manner of speaking, they announced in advance his arrival. I like to think of them as *pre-echoes*. Since the voice and actions of Jesus on earth transcended space and time, they must have reverberated both before and after their time.

If this is getting a bit too philosophical, let me just point out that, if we look closely, we can see the promises of Jesus reflected in many of the promises given in the Old Testament as well as in the lives of some Old Testament characters. As the book of Hebrews illustrates, the words and promises of the Old Testament are alive, and we are wise if we hear God's voice today and not harden our hearts (Hebrews 3:7-8).

SUNDAY: I'm Surrounded by Love

Lord, today I lift up prayer for:

Date: _____ Names: _____

(Use the following space for future weeks when you cycle again through these prayers.)

Date: _____ Names: _____

Date: _____ Names: _____

Date: _____ Names: _____

Date: _____ Names: _____

Scriptures

Sunday's key promise from Jesus:

> "Surely I am with you always, to the very end of the age" (Matthew 28:20).

Supportive promise from Scripture:

> "I will not forget you! See, I have engraved you on the palms of my hands" (Isaiah 49:15b-16a).

Daily Prayer Opener

(See page 124)

Promise Prayer

Lord,

It's Sunday, so I'm Surrounded by your love. Today I desire to dig deeper, through prayer, into the reality of your presence in our lives. I will do this by praying other Scriptures from the Old Testament that reflect your promise to be with us always.

Be for us, as you were for Moses and the Israelites, a pillar of cloud by day and a pillar of fire at night, always in front of us showing the way.

Lord, as you said to Jacob in his dream at Bethel, so I ask you to be with us and watch over us wherever we go. Please do not leave us until you have done what you have promised. Hold tight to your pledge and remind us that, just as you were with Jacob, you are surely in this place with us today.

And I pray that when we cannot feel your presence, our eyes would be opened, like Elisha's servant, to see that those who are with us are more than those who are against us. Help us discern that your angels are guarding us, and they will lift us up in their hands and we will dwell in the shelter of the Most High.

In the name of Immanuel, God-with-us, I pray. Amen.

> Genesis 28:15-16; Psalm 139:1-3,7; 2 Kings 6:16; Psalm 91:1,11-12; Deuteronomy 7:9; Exodus 13:21

MONDAY: I'm Making Happiness a Habit

Lord, today I lift up prayer for:

Date: _____ Names: _____

(Use the following space for future weeks when you cycle again through these prayers.)

Date: _____ Names: _____

Date: _____ Names: _____

Date: _____ Names: _____

Date: _____ Names: _____

Scriptures

Monday's key promise from Jesus:

> "I have told you this so that my joy may be in you and that
> your joy may be complete" (John 15:11).

Supportive promise from Scripture:

> "This is the day which the LORD has made;
> Let us rejoice and be glad in it."
> (Psalm 118:24 NASB)

Daily Prayer Opener

(See page 124)

Promise Prayer

Lord,

It's Monday, so I'm Making happiness a habit. Today I want to dig deeper, through prayer, into the reality of your joy in our lives. I will do this by praying other Scriptures from the Old Testament that reflect your promises of joy and gladness.

Lord, your Word says a cheerful heart is good medicine, so today I pray that our hearts will be filled with laughter, just as Sarah experienced when Isaac was born. In the same way, may you bring laughter and happiness into our hearts today.

As David leaped and danced before you with all his might, I pray that our wailing be turned into dancing and that our sackcloth be removed. I ask you to clothe us with joy so that our hearts may sing to you and not be silent.

Lord, your words are our joy and our hearts' delight. We want to shout aloud and sing for joy, for you are the great and Holy One. Satisfy us in the morning with your unfailing love.

Allow us to sing for joy and be glad all our days. For this is the day you have made; we will rejoice and be glad in it.

In the joyful name of Jesus, I pray. Amen.

> Proverbs 17:22a; Genesis 21:6; Ecclesiastes 3:4; Jeremiah 15:16; Isaiah 12:6; Habakkuk 3:18-19; 2 Samuel 6:14-16; Psalm 30:11-12; 90:14; 118:24

TUESDAY: I'm Trusting in God's Strength

Lord, today I lift up prayer for:

Date: _____ Names: _____

(Use the following space for future weeks when you cycle again through these prayers.)

Date: _____ Names: _____

Date: _____ Names: _____

Date: _____ Names: _____

Date: _____ Names: _____

Scriptures

Tuesday's key promise from Jesus:

> "Truly I tell you, if you have faith as small as a mustard seed, you can say to this mountain, 'Move from here to there,' and it will move. Nothing will be impossible for you" (Matthew 17:20-21).

Supportive promise from Scripture:

> "The LORD is my strength and my shield;
>   my heart trusts in him, and he helps me."
>   (Psalm 28:7)

Daily Prayer Opener

(See page 124)

Promise Prayer

Lord,

It's Tuesday, so I'm Trusting in your strength today. I want to dig deeper, through prayer, into the power of your strength in our lives. I will do this by praying other Scriptures from the Old Testament that reflect your promise to be our strength.

Lord, you are God Almighty. Everything in heaven and earth is yours, and you have the power to exalt and give strength to all. You arm us with strength and make our way perfect. You broaden the path beneath us so that our ankles do not turn. You uphold us when we fall and lift us up when we are bowed down.

I confess, though, that sometimes we feel like Solomon, that everything is meaningless, utterly meaningless. In those times, help us to stop and realize that as we know not the path of the wind, so too we cannot understand your works, O God, the maker of all things.

Lord, you are the stronghold of our life and our soul finds rest in you alone. Our hope comes from you, for you are our rock and our salvation; you are our fortress and we will not be shaken.

In the strong name of Jesus, I pray. Amen.

> 1 Chronicles 29:11-12; 2 Samuel 22:33,37; Psalm 39:7; 145:14; Jeremiah 17:7; Proverbs 23:18; Ecclesiastes 1:2; 11:5; Psalm 27:1; 62:5-6

WEDNESDAY: I'm Wanting What God Wants

Lord, today I lift up prayer for:

Date: _____ Names: _____

(Use the following space for future weeks when you cycle again through these prayers.)

Date: _____ Names: _____

Date: _____ Names: _____

Date: _____ Names: _____

Date: _____ Names: _____

Scriptures

Wednesday's key promise from Jesus:

> "You may ask me for anything in my name, and I will do it" (John 14:14).

Supportive promise from Scripture:

> "'For my thoughts are not your thoughts,
>   neither are your ways my ways,' declares the LORD."
>   (Isaiah 55:8)

Daily Prayer Opener

(See page 124)

Promise Prayer

Lord,

It's Wednesday, so I'm Wanting what you want today. I desire to dig deeper, through prayer, into the excellence of your will in our lives. I will do this by praying other Scriptures from the Old Testament that reflect your promise to guide us always.

Just as the people came to Moses to seek God's will, we come to you, Lord. We know that you alone are God, who makes known the end from the beginning, from ancient times, what is still to come. Your purpose will stand, and what you have planned you will do.

Along with Micah, I confess that you have shown us what is good and what you require of us—to act justly, to love mercy, and to walk humbly with you, O God. You esteem those who are humble and contrite in spirit, who tremble at your Word.

Lord, sometimes we lose sleep and pace back and forth worrying about which direction we should go in our lives. So I ask you today, please show us your will. Help us trust and love you with all our heart and soul. Your Word says that when you delight in our ways, you will make our steps firm. Though we stumble we will not fall, and you will uphold us with your hand.

In the name of Jesus, who wanted the Father's will above all. Amen.

> Psalm 37:23-24; 138:8; Deuteronomy 13:3-4; Exodus 18:15;
> Isaiah 46:10-11; 66:2; Psalm 90:12,17; Deuteronomy 5:32-33

THURSDAY: I'm Trading My Troubles for Peace

Lord, today I lift up prayer for:

Date: _____ Names: _____

(Use the following space for future weeks when you cycle again through these prayers.)

Date: _____ Names: _____

Date: _____ Names: _____

Date: _____ Names: _____

Date: _____ Names: _____

Scriptures

Thursday's key promise from Jesus:

> "Come to me, all you who are weary and burdened, and I
> will give you rest" (Matthew 11:28).

Supportive promise from Scripture:

> "In peace I will lie down and sleep,
>   for you alone, LORD,
>   make me dwell in safety."
>   (Psalm 4:8)

Daily Prayer Opener

(See page 124)

Promise Prayer

Lord,

It's Thursday, so I'm Trading my troubles for peace. Today I
desire to dig deeper, through prayer, into your peace that
passes understanding. I will do this by praying Scriptures
from the Old Testament that reflect your promise to give us
peace.

Lord, when we are afraid, we will trust in you. When we are filled
with worry, help us remember that you give great peace to
those who love your law, and nothing can make them stumble. You have promised that though the mountains be shaken
and the hills be removed, your unfailing love for us will not
tremble nor your covenant of peace be revoked. Though our
flesh and heart may fail, you are our strength.

Help us remember the blessing you bestowed upon the Israelites: "The LORD bless you and keep you; the LORD make his face shine on you and be gracious to you; the LORD turn his face toward you and give you peace." Teach us that better are those who have one handful with tranquility than two handfuls with toil and chasing after the wind.

And may we never forget that you sent your Suffering Servant, who took up our infirmities and carried our sorrows. He was pierced for our transgressions, crushed for our iniquities, and given the punishment that brought us peace. Hallelujah—by his wounds we are healed.

In the name of the Suffering Servant, Jesus, I pray. Amen.

> Psalm 25:17; 56:3; 119:165; Isaiah 54:10; Psalm 73:26;
> 1 Chronicles 28:20; Ecclesiastes 4:6; Numbers 6:22-26; Isaiah 53:4-5

FRIDAY: I'm Finding Freedom

Lord, today I lift up prayer for:

Date: _____ Names: _____

(Use the following space for future weeks when you cycle again through these prayers.)

Date: _____ Names: _____

Date: _____ Names: _____

Date: _____ Names: _____

Date: _____ Names: _____

Date: _____ Names: _____

Date: _____ Names: _____

Scriptures

Friday's key promise from Jesus:

> "If the Son sets you free, you will be free indeed" (John 8:36).

Supportive promise from Scripture:

> "I will walk about in freedom,
>> for I have sought out your precepts."
>> (Psalm 119:45)

Daily Prayer Opener

(See page 124)

Promise Prayer

Lord,

It's Friday, so I'm Finding freedom today. I want to dig deeper, through prayer, into the liberty you have given us. I will do this by praying Scriptures from the Old Testament that reflect your promise to set us free.

O Lord, we are your servants for you have freed us from our chains. We are pure and clean and free from sin because of your grace. Your mercy is new every morning—great is your faithfulness.

Lord, from you comes deliverance, for you have said to those in darkness, "Come out and be free!" As David cried out to you from the cave, we cry out for release from our hiding places. And as you said to the Israelites, "I am the LORD, and I will free you from being slaves, and I will redeem you with an outstretched arm," O Lord, redeem us.

Yet sometimes, Lord, we feel oppressed and influenced by the evil one, and our thoughts and actions seem to be held captive by this foe. I call out to you, Lord, to save us from our enemies.

Even in our old age, you are God and will sustain us, for you made us and will rescue us.

In the freeing name of Jesus, I pray. Amen.

> Psalm 116:6; Job 33:9; Lamentations 3:22-23; Psalm 142:7; Exodus 6:6-7; Psalm 3:8; Isaiah 49:9; Proverbs 11:21; Isaiah 49:23b; 2 Samuel 22:4; Isaiah 46:4

SATURDAY: I'm So Excited About Heaven

Lord, today I lift up prayer for:

Date: _____ Names: _____

(Use the following space for future weeks when you cycle again through these prayers.)

Date: _____ Names: _____

Date: _____ Names: _____

Date: _____ Names: _____

Date: _____ Names: _____

Scriptures

Saturday's key promise from Jesus:

> "In My Father's house are many dwelling places; if it were not so, I would have told you; for I go to prepare a place for you" (John 14:2 NASB).

Supportive promise from Scripture:

> "He has also set eternity in the human heart" (Ecclesiastes 3:11).

Daily Prayer Opener

(See page 124)

Promise Prayer

Lord,

It's Saturday, and I'm So excited about heaven. Today I desire to dig deeper, through prayer, into the promises of life eternal with you. I will do this by praying Scriptures from the Old Testament that reflect your promise of everlasting life.

Lord, you have looked down from heaven and viewed the earth, and have determined our days. You have decreed the number of our months and set limits we cannot exceed. May we enjoy each day as your gift to us, for this is the day you have made.

We pray today that we can be like Nebuchadnezzar, who raised his eyes toward heaven and praised the Most High. He honored and glorified you because you live forever, whereas even kings live only for a short time and then are forgotten. Your dominion is eternal, and your kingdom endures from generation to generation.

Lord, you have promised that you will create a new heaven and a new earth, that the former things will not be remembered nor will they come to mind. We rejoice in what you will create, for it will be a delight and the sound of weeping and crying will be heard no more. Surely goodness and love will follow us all the days of our lives, and we will dwell in your house forever.

In the eternal name of Jesus, I pray. Amen.

2 Kings 2:3,12; Psalm 102:19,25,27-28; Job 14:5; Psalm 118:24; Daniel 4:34; Isaiah 65:17-19; Psalm 23:6

15

WEEK FOUR

Praying the Promises of Jesus as Reflected in the New Testament

"Let us hold unswervingly to the hope we profess, for he who promised is faithful."

Hebrews 10:23

SUNDAY: I'm Surrounded by Love

Lord, today I lift up prayer for:

Date: _____ Names: _____

(Use the following space for future weeks when you cycle again through these prayers.)

Date: _____ Names: _____

Date: _____ Names: _____

Date: _____ Names: _____

Date: _____ Names: _____

Scriptures

Sunday's key promise from Jesus:

> "Surely I am with you always, to the very end of the age" (Matthew 28:20).

Supportive promise from Scripture:

> "This is how we know that we live in him and he in us: He has given us of his Spirit" (1 John 4:13).

Daily Prayer Opener
(See page 124)

Promise Prayer
Lord,

Today is Sunday, so I'm Surrounded by your love. Today I desire to dig deeper, through prayer, into the reality of your presence in our lives. I will do this by praying other Scriptures from the New Testament that reflect your promise to be with us always.

Lord, as you were preparing to leave this earth you promised to send another Counselor to be with us forever, the Spirit of truth, who will live with us and be in us. Thank you for not leaving us alone, and that through the Holy Spirit you are with us and in us.

Help us to know, like the widows in Timothy's church who were in need, that we can put our hope in you and pray night and day, asking for help. Thank you for promising that when we draw near to you, you will draw near to us. Lord, remind us when we are frightened, as you said to Paul, "Do not be afraid...for I am with you." When the storms of life seem about to drown us, may we hear your voice, as you said to the disciples, "It is I; don't be afraid."

We remember with awe that even you, Lord Jesus, felt alone at times: when you prayed alone in the Garden of Gethsemane, when you were betrayed by a follower, when you were rejected by a friend, when you were mocked and beaten, and when you cried from the cross, "My God, my God, why have you forsaken me?" In spite of these feelings, you said, "I am not alone, for my Father is with me." In the same way, may we know today that though we may feel alone, the reality is that we are never alone and you are with us.

In Jesus' comforting name I pray. Amen.

> John 14:16-17; 1 Timothy 5:5; James 4:8; Acts 18:9-10; John 6:20; Luke 15:20; John 14:3; Mark 14:32-51; Luke 22:54-62; John 19:1-6; Matthew 27:45; John 16:32

MONDAY: I'm Making Happiness a Habit

Lord, today I lift up prayer for:

Date: _____ Names: _____

(Use the following space for future weeks when you cycle again through these prayers.)

Date: _____ Names: _____

Date: _____ Names: _____

Date: _____ Names: _____

Date: _____ Names: _____

Scriptures

Monday's key promise from Jesus:

> "I have told you this so that my joy may be in you and that your joy may be complete" (John 15:11).

Supportive promise from Scripture:

> "Rejoice in the Lord always. I will say it again: Rejoice!" (Philippians 4:4).

Daily Prayer Opener

(See page 124)

Promise Prayer

Lord,

It's Monday, so I'm Making happiness a habit.

Your Word says, "Is anyone of you in trouble? He should pray. Is anyone happy? Let him sing songs of praise." Because of this, we ask you to overflow our hearts today with happiness and praise. As Mary sang when she carried the baby Jesus, "My soul glorifies the Lord and my spirit rejoices in God my Savior...for the Mighty One has done great things for me—holy is his name," so too our souls glorify you today, Lord, and our spirits rejoice.

Lord Jesus, throughout your life on earth, you brought joy to people. At your birth, the angel said, "Do not be afraid, I bring you good news of great joy that will be for all the people." During your triumphant entry, the crowds joyfully praised God in loud voices for the miracles they had seen. And after your resurrection, the disciples worshipped you and returned to Jerusalem with great joy. In the same way, I pray that you would bring joy into our lives throughout our days. May our hearts be filled with happiness and joy today as we trust that our lives are in your hands.

In your blessed name, I pray. Amen.

> James 5:13; Luke 1:46-47; John 16:22-24; Luke 2:10; 15:10; 19:37-38; 24:52; Acts 2:26-28

TUESDAY: I'm Trusting in God's Strength

Lord, today I lift up prayer for:

Date: _____ Names: _____

(Use the following space for future weeks when you cycle again through these prayers.)

Date: _____ Names: _____

Date: _____ Names: _____

Date: _____ Names: _____

Date: _____ Names: _____

Scriptures

Tuesday's key promise from Jesus:

> "Truly I tell you, if you have faith as small as a mustard seed, you can say to this mountain, 'Move from here to there,' and it will move. Nothing will be impossible for you" (Matthew 17:20-21).

Supportive promise from Scripture:

> "For Christ's sake, I delight in weaknesses...for when I am weak, then I am strong" (2 Corinthians 12:10).

Daily Prayer Opener

(See page 124)

Promise Prayer

Lord,

It's Tuesday, so I'm Trusting in your strength today.

Lord, our faith is so weak at times. Yet your Word reminds us that you were crucified in weakness yet live by God's power.

Likewise, we are weak yet also live by God's power. We are so grateful that we have a high priest who is able to sympathize with our weaknesses, so we can approach the throne of grace with confidence in our times of need. Thank you for sending the Holy Spirit to help us when we are weak, for we often don't even know how to pray, but the Spirit intercedes for us with groans that words cannot express.

Lord, I pray that out of your glorious riches you may strengthen us with power through your Spirit in our inner being, so we may be filled to the measure of all the fullness of God. Thank you for not giving us a spirit of timidity, but a spirit of power, love, and self-discipline.

We know that nothing is impossible with you, God, so today we pray that we could take hold of the hope offered to us and be greatly encouraged. Your hope is an anchor to our soul, firm and secure.

With a hopeful heart I pray. Amen.

> 2 Corinthians 13:4; Romans 8:26; Hebrews 4:15-16; Ephesians 3:16-19; 2 Timothy 1:7; Luke 1:37; Hebrews 6:18-19; 2 Corinthians 1:8-10

WEDNESDAY: I'm Wanting What God Wants

Lord, today I lift up prayer for:

Date: _____ Names: _____

(Use the following space for future weeks when you cycle again through these prayers.)

Date: _____ Names: _____

Date: _____ Names: _____

Date: _____ Names: _____

Date: _____ Names: _____

Scriptures

Wednesday's key promise from Jesus:

> "You may ask me for anything in my name, and I will do it" (John 14:14).

Supportive promise from Scripture:

> "For it is God who works in you to will and to act in order to fulfill his good purpose" (Philippians 2:13).

Daily Prayer Opener

(See page 124)

Promise Prayer

Lord,

It's Wednesday, so I'm Wanting what you want.

Thank you for coming down from heaven not to do your will but the will of him who sent you. For your Father's will is that everyone who looks to you and believes in you shall have eternal life. You asked us to go and make disciples of all nations, baptizing them in the name of the Father and of the Son and of the Holy Spirit, and teaching them to obey everything you commanded. Lord, I pray that we can be ambassadors of your love and grace to our family, friends, community, and world.

Lord, I pray we can be like the wise builder and build our lives on the solid foundation. When the floods come, our lives will be well-built and cannot be shaken. Also, help us to not be like the person who built on sand. When the storms strike, such lives collapse and their destruction is complete.

Lord, we desire to follow you today, and I pray that you would equip us with everything we need to do your will, to accomplish what pleases you. May our hearts learn and apply all that you teach us each day, and may our spirits be humbled and diligent as we follow you.

In your victorious name, I pray. Amen.

> John 6:28-29,38-40; Hebrews 13:20-21; Luke 6:46-49; Matthew 28:19-20a

THURSDAY: I'm Trading My Troubles for Peace

Lord, today I lift up prayer for:

Date: _____ Names: _____

(Use the following space for future weeks when you cycle again through these prayers.)

Date: _____ Names: _____

Date: _____ Names: _____

Date: _____ Names: _____

Date: _____ Names: _____

Scriptures

Thursday's key promise from Jesus:

> "Come to me, all you who are weary and burdened, and I will give you rest" (Matthew 11:28).

Supportive promise from Scripture:

> "Now may the Lord of peace himself give you peace at all times and in every way. The Lord be with you all" (2 Thessalonians 3:16).

Daily Prayer Opener

(See page 124)

Promise Prayer

Lord,

It's Thursday, so I'm Trading my troubles for peace today.

Lord, though we face difficulties each day, remind us that our present sufferings are not worth comparing with the glory that will be revealed in us. Please give us peace in our sufferings and help us trust in the future you have for us.

Lord, we are weary with worries and fears. How comforting it is to read in your Word that Paul also struggled. Even more, he discovered that you, the God of all comfort, brought him relief from all his difficulties. Lord, we also are tired and weary, but you have promised a Sabbath rest for your people. You have promised that those who enter your rest also rest from their work, just as you did from yours. Help us enter into your rest today.

Lord, a woman once came to you, a woman who had suffered physically for years. She realized that a mere touch of your clothes would heal her, and immediately after touching you, it was so. You said to her, "Daughter, your faith has healed you. Go in peace and be freed from your suffering." Lord, like this woman of faith, may you give us the faith and courage to also bring our needs to you, and may we be healed and find peace in your presence.

In your healing name, I pray. Amen.

Romans 8:18; 2 Corinthians 1:3-4; 7:5-6; Hebrews 4:8-11; Mark 5:25-34

FRIDAY: I'm Finding Freedom

Lord, today I lift up prayer for:

Date: _____ Names: _____

(Use the following space for future weeks when you cycle again through these prayers.)

Date: _____ Names: _____

Date: _____ Names: _____

Date: _____ Names: _____

Date: _____ Names: _____

Scriptures

Friday's key promise from Jesus:

> "If the Son sets you free, you will be free indeed" (John 8:36).

Supportive promise from Scripture:

> "It is for freedom that Christ has set us free" (Galatians 5:1).

Daily Prayer Opener

(See page 124)

Promise Prayer

Lord,

It's Friday, so I'm Finding freedom today.

Lord, your Word teaches us that creation itself will be liberated from its bondage to decay and brought into the glorious freedom of God, so we wait patiently for this hope of liberation. One day our earthly bonds will be broken, and we will find freedom beyond our wildest dreams.

Lord, through faith we are able to approach you with freedom and confidence. You have rescued us from the dominion of darkness and brought us into your kingdom, and in you we have redemption and the forgiveness of sins. Therefore, we choose to live as free people, but we will not use our freedom as an excuse for evil, but we will live as your servants.

We realize, Lord, that we can either be slaves to sin, which leads to death, or slaves to obedience, which leads to righteousness. Thanks be to you, O God, for though we were slaves to sin, we have been set free from sin and have become slaves to righteousness. Because of this, the benefits we reap lead to holiness, and the result is eternal life.

In your liberating name, I pray. Amen.

> Romans 8:20; Ephesians 3:12; Colossians 1:13-14; 1 Peter 2:16; Romans 6:16-17,22; Luke 4:16-21

SATURDAY: I'm So Excited About Heaven

Lord, today I lift up prayer for:

Date: _____ Names: _____

(Use the following space for future weeks when you cycle again through these prayers.)

Date: _____ Names: _____

Date: _____ Names: _____

Date: _____ Names: _____

Date: _____ Names: _____

Scriptures

Saturday's key promise from Jesus:

> "In My Father's house are many dwelling places; if it were
> not so, I would have told you; for I go to prepare a place
> for you" (John 14:2 NASB).

Supportive promise from Scripture:

> "Repent, for the kingdom of heaven has come near" (Mat-
> thew 4:17).

Daily Prayer Opener

(See page 124)

Promise Prayer

Lord,

It's Saturday, and I'm So excited about heaven.

Lord, as Stephen, full of the Holy Spirit, looked up to heaven
and saw the glory of God and you, Jesus, standing at the right
hand of the Father, may we know that one day we will see
the heavens open and you in your glory. As the prodigal son
was welcomed home by his father, who ran to him, threw his
arms around him, and kissed him, we look forward to that
day when you welcome us to our eternal homes. For you have
promised you are now preparing a place for us. Like the thief
on the cross, we will be with you in paradise.

Lord, we look forward to the day when we hear you say, "Come,
you who are blessed by my Father, take your inheritance, the
kingdom prepared for you since the creation of the world."
Like Abraham, we are looking forward to the city with foundations, whose architect and builder is God. We long to rest
beside the river of life and eat from the tree that yields fruit
every month. We yearn to worship before the throne of grace
and see the face of the Lamb. We are so excited to be able to

dwell together with the community of saints in a place without darkness, for you will give us light. We can't begin to fathom what it means to reign with you forever and ever, but we look forward to serving however you see fit.

Lord, we know that our bodies, the earthly tents in which we live, will be destroyed. But they will be replaced with heavenly bodies and eternal homes not built by human hands. We pray for great patience as we wait for all of this to occur. At the end of the age you will send out your angels, will call us to heaven, and the righteous will shine like the sun in the kingdom of the Father. Because of you and you alone, we will be confident and unashamed before you at your coming.

Marana-tha! Come, Lord Jesus! Amen.

> Luke 15:20; Acts 7:55-56; Luke 23:43; John 3:13-15; Matthew 25:34; Hebrews 11:10; Revelation 22:1-5; 2 Corinthians 5:1-5; Matthew 13:40-43; 1 John 2:28

APPENDIX

Daily Prayer Themes
and Key Scriptures

Sunday: I'm Surrounded by love.

> Key verse: "Surely I am with you always, to the very end of the age" (Matthew 28:20).

Monday: I'm Making happiness a habit.

> Key verse: "I have told you this so that my joy may be in you and that your joy may be complete" (John 15:11).

Tuesday: I'm Trusting in God's strength.

> Key verse: "Truly I tell you, if you have faith as small as a mustard seed, you can say to this mountain, 'Move from here to there,' and it will move. Nothing will be impossible for you" (Matthew 17:20-21).

Wednesday: I'm Wanting what God wants.

> Key verse: "You may ask me for anything in my name, and I will do it" (John 14:14).

Thursday: I'm Trading my troubles for peace.

> Key verse: "Come to me, all you who are weary and burdened, and I will give you rest" (Matthew 11:28).

Friday: I'm Finding freedom.

> Key verse: "If the Son sets you free, you will be free indeed" (John 8:36).

Saturday: I'm So excited about heaven.

> Key verse: "In My Father's house are many dwelling places; if it were not so, I would have told you; for I go to prepare a place for you" (John 14:2 NASB).

Notes

1. The Greatest Promise-Maker of All Time

1. Three prayers in the Bible are often assumed to be silent prayers: the prayer of Abraham's servant in Genesis 24:10-15; Hannah's prayer in 1 Samuel 1:9-16; and Nehemiah's prayer in Nehemiah 2:1-5. None of the three cases, however, mentions that the prayer was given in silence, so to hold these to be examples of silent prayer is to make, ironically, an argument from silence. This criticism also applies to those who assume Jesus' instruction for prayer in Matthew 6:6 refers only to silent prayer: "But when you pray, go into your room, close the door and pray to your Father, who is unseen. Then your Father, who sees what is done in secret, will reward you." In this verse, silent prayer certainly is permitted but not mandated.

   Concerning Hannah's prayer, some readers assume she was praying in silence. Instead, I think a case can be made that her moving lips imply she was speaking very quietly, so much so that Eli could not hear her. We might call this a "whisper prayer." In any event, moving one's lips in prayer is still an embodied prayer rather than merely mental.

2. The Power of Promises

1. I heard this phrase from Lewis Smedes in an ethics class at Fuller Theological Seminary in 1981 (where I had the privilege of knowing Dr. Smedes as a professor and friend). In print, he put the same thought this way: "I create a small island of certainty for you in the swirling waters of our uncertainties: it is the certainty of my presence with you." Lewis B. Smedes, *Caring and Commitment: Learning to Live the Love We Promise* (San Francisco: Harper and Row, Publishers, 1988), 5. In a later chapter, Smedes credited Hannah Arendt as the originator of both this concept and phraseology in her book *The Human Condition*. See Smedes, *Caring and Commitment*, 147.

3. How Promises Create Relationships

1. James MacDonald, *Always True: God's 5 Promises When Life Is Hard* (Chicago: Moody Publishers, 2011), 12.

2. The Old Testament is sometimes called the covenant of law in opposition to the New Testament that is seen as the covenant of grace. However, the phrase "covenant of law" never occurs in the Old Testament, whereas the phrase "covenant of love" occurs at least seven times (Deuteronomy 7:9, 7:12; 1 Kings 8:23; 2 Chronicles 6:14; Nehemiah 1:5; 9:32; Daniel 9:4). Might Christians value the Old Testament more if they viewed its covenant through a love rather than law lens?

3. Does this mean that divorce is never allowed for Christians? No, for Moses, Jesus, and Paul all outlined acceptable reasons for divorce. But these are limited and specific, as opposed to today's secular, no-fault rationale for divorce.

4. Sunday: I'm Surrounded by Love

1. Pun intended.

2. Gwen Costello, *Spiritual Gems from Mother Teresa* (New London, CT: Twenty-third Publications, 2008), 20.

3. Quoted in John Ortberg, *Everybody's Normal Till You Get to Know Them* (Grand Rapids, MI: Zondervan, 2003), 30.

4. Thomas Wolfe, *The Hills Beyond* (Baton Rouge, LA: Louisiana State Univ. Press, 1935, 2000), 186.

5. Skeptics sometimes ask, "How could there be a 'before' before time itself was created?" The problem is one of language: in our time-dominated mindset, words fail to properly express what reality was like before time itself was created. God, as the creator of all physical and temporal reality, that is, the space-time continuum, must have existed in his own reality beyond time.

6. This is based on many such promises of God in the Old Testament: Genesis 28:15; Deuteronomy 31:6; Joshua 1:5; 1 Kings 6:13; 1 Chronicles 28:20; Isaiah 42:16; and Isaiah 43:1-2,4-5, which so beautifully reads:

> But now, this is what the LORD says—
> he who created you, Jacob,
> he who formed you, Israel:
> "Do not fear, for I have redeemed you;
> I have summoned you by name; you are mine.
> When you pass through the waters,
> I will be with you;
> and when you pass through the rivers,
> they will not sweep over you.
> When you walk through the fire,
> you will not be burned...
> Since you are precious and honored in my sight,
> and because I love you...
> Do not be afraid, for I am with you."

7. Thomas Olden, ed., *Saint Patrick: The Epistles and Hymns of St. Patrick* (Dublin: Hodges, Foster and Co., 1876), 109.

8. Teenagers, for instance, are said to send over one hundred texts per day, on average. www.nielsen.com/us/en/insights/news/2010/u-s-teen-mobile-report-calling-yesterday-texting-today-using-apps-tomorrow.html, accessed 1/26/2015.

5. Monday: I'm Making Happiness a Habit

1. William Barclay, *Daily Study Bible: Luke, The King's Banquet and the King's Guests (Luke 14:15-24)*, www.studylight.org/commentaries/dsb/view.cgi?bk=41&ch=14 (accessed 2-25-2015).

2. Pamela Gerloff, "You're Not Laughing Enough, and That's No Joke," *Psychology Today*, June 21, 2011, www.psychologytoday.com/blog/the-possibility-paradigm/201106/youre-not-laughing-enough-and-thats-no-joke, (accessed 1-21-2015). Dr. Gerloff holds a doctorate in human development from Harvard University.

3. Blaise Pascal, *Thoughts, Letters, Minor Works* (New York: P.F. Collier and Son, 1910), 138.

4. Henry David Thoreau, *Walden* (New York: New American Library of World Literature, 1960), 10.

5. "Blessed" is translated "happy" in several translations of the Beatitudes in Matthew 5:3-12, such as the J.B. Phillips New Testament, the Common English Bible, the Good News Translation, the Living Bible, the New Life Version, the Worldwide English New Testament, and Young's Literal Translation.

6. Gerhard Kittel, Gerhard Friedrich, and Geoffrey W. Bromley, eds., "*Makarios*," *Theological Dictionary of the New Testament, Abridged in One Volume* (Grand Rapids, MI: Wm. B. Eerdmans Publishing Co., 1985), 548-49.

7. Several of the biblical words for joy are very active words at root level, including *happiness, exultation, gladness, delight,* and even *dancing.* James Strong, *"1523" Strong's Exhaustive Concordance, Hebrew and Chaldee Dictionary Appendix* (Peabody, MA: Hendrickson Publishers, 2007).

8. *Today in the Word,* June 1988, 13.

9. Mark Jones, *Echoes of Heaven* (Joplin, MO: Heartspring Publishing, 2003), 34.

10. Norman Cousins is well known for adopting what he termed "laughter therapy" and "inner jogging" after medical efforts were ineffective on his chronic disease. Norman Cousins, *Anatomy of an Illness* (New York: W.W. Norton, 1979), 94.

6. Tuesday: I'm Trusting in God's Strength

1. Quoted in Debbie Taylor, *Pray with Purpose, Live with Passion* (West Monroe, LA: Howard Publishing, 2006), 37.

2. Quoted in Phillip Yancey, *Reaching for the Invisible God* (Grand Rapids, MI: Zondervan, 2000), 42.

3. From the sermon, "Why Jesus Called a Man a Fool," delivered at Mount Pisgah Missionary Baptist Church on August 27, 1967, in Chicago, Illinois, https://kinginstitute.stanford.edu/king-papers/publications/knock-midnight-inspiration-great-sermons-reverend-martin-luther-king-jr-7 (accessed January 27, 2015).

4. Lilian Kwan, "John Piper Reflects on 30-Year Ministry," *The Christian Post,* December 11, 2012. www.christianpost.com/news/john-piper-reflects-on-30-year-ministry-warns-pastors-to-avoid-stereotypes-86491 (accessed February 20, 2015).

5. Ray C. Stedman, "The Holy Spirit and Prayer," a sermon preached at Peninsula Bible Church in Palo Alto, California, on April 19, 1964. www.raystedman.org/thematic-studies/prayer/the-holy-spirit-and-prayer (accessed December 7, 2014).

6. Ibid.

7. *The Collected Works of G.K. Chesterton, Vol. 1* (San Francisco: Ignatius Press, 1986), 125, 100.

7. Wednesday: I'm Wanting What God Wants

1. C.S. Lewis, *The Great Divorce* (New York: Harper Collins, 1946), 75.

2. Some proponents of aggressive prayer counsel against saying to God, "if it is your will." They feel it reveals doubt rather than faith and weakens the power of assertive prayer. In my opinion, the opposite is true: appending "if it is your will" to a prayer request is evidence of humility, not doubt. It cannot inhibit God's power, and it won't change his will. "Come near to God and he will come near to you...Humble yourselves before the Lord, and he will lift you up" (James 4:8a, 10).

3. Since the name Stedman is extremely rare, well-read Christians often assume that I am the son of Ray Stedman, the well-known pastor and author from Palo Alto, California, who was very popular in the seventies and eighties. Though Ray and I were not, as far as I know, relatives, I was able to meet him on two occasions before his passing. Both times he seemed genuinely happy to meet another Stedman. Twice he put his hand on my shoulder and said, "At least you spell your name right." I wish I could talk with him again, this time about the meaning of our common name: that it means to stand in the place of another. I believe this would have delighted Ray, because he clearly understood this as the core meaning to praying in Jesus' name.

4. Ray C. Stedman, "The Holy Spirit and Prayer," a sermon preached at Peninsula Bible Church in Palo Alto, California, on April 19, 1964. www.raystedman.org/thematic-studies/prayer/the-holy-spirit-and-prayer (accessed December 7, 2014).

5. Curtis C. Mitchell, *Praying Jesus' Way* (Old Tappan, NJ: Fleming H. Revell Company, 1977), 109-10.

6. Ray Stedman comments, "I know there are some Christians who are very troubled by the idea that there ever was a time when Jesus did not want to do the Father's will, and they are upset when you suggest this...[One such person said] Jesus' statement, 'Not my will, but thine,' is the acme of perfect and voluntary submission on his part. It is. Jesus does want to do the Father's will, ultimately, and he does choose to obey. But the language is evacuated of its content if you take out all the sense of division and conflict that is in these words...Something within [Jesus] made him dread it, and we can understand why he did not want to go ahead, why he wanted to escape it." Ray C. Stedman, "Smite the Shepherd," sermon at Peninsula Bible Church in Palo Alto, California, September 14, 1975. www.pbc.org/system/message_files/4128/3327.html (accessed February 5, 2015).

7. Richard Foster, *Prayer: Finding the Heart's True Home* (San Francisco: Harper Collins, 1992), 49.

8. Andrew Murray, quoted in Foster, *Prayer*, 49.

9. I believe the apostle Paul, when he was told by eyewitnesses the events of Jesus' life, found this expression to be poignant and powerful. This is because the phrase, "Abba, Father," appears only two other times in the New Testament in letters written by Paul (Romans 8:15 and Galatians 4:6).

10. This verse is very dear to me. When asked what verse best sums up the life of a megachurch pastor, I always quote this one.

11. Foster, *Prayer*, 53.

12. N.T. Wright, *The Way of the Lord* (Grand Rapids, MI: Wm. B. Eerdmans Publishing Co., 1999), 90.

13. Franklin Graham and Jeanette Lockerbie, *Bob Pierce: This One Thing I Do* (Waco, TX: Word Books, 1983).

8. Thursday: I'm Trading My Troubles for Peace

1. Soren Kierkegaard, *Training in Christianity* (New York: Vintage Books, 2004), 6.

2. Matthew 6:25,31,34; 10:19; Mark 13:11; Luke 12:11,22,29; 21:14.

3. Like Paul in Ephesians 3:8, I see myself as the least of the saints.

4. Quoted in Max Lucado, *Life to the Full* (Nashville, TN: Thomas Nelson Publishers, 2005), 48.

5. A third spiritual discipline to help overcome worry is to develop vulnerability and deep trust in an accountability group with mature believers. Prayer, in such a context, can significantly put at ease our worrisome thoughts.

6. Rick Stedman, *Praying the Armor of God* (Eugene, OR: Harvest House Publishers, 2015), 37-41.

7. Matthew 27:34.

9. Friday: I'm Finding Freedom

1. Mario Cuomo and Harold Holzer, eds., *Lincoln on Democracy* (New York: Fordham University Press, 2004), 343.

2. It is easy to assume that "Be fruitful and multiply" (Genesis 1:28 NASB) were God's first words to Adam because they are found in the first chapter of Genesis rather than the second. But the context of the verse reveals that these words were spoken to both Adam and Eve: "God blessed *them;* and God said to *them*, 'Be fruitful and multiply.'" The words recorded in Genesis 2:16,

"You are free," are said to Adam only, before Eve was created. Hence, Genesis 2:16 occurred before Genesis 1:28.

3. John Steinbeck, *East of Eden* (New York: Penguin Group, 2002), 301.

4. Henry Cloud and John Townsend, *Boundaries* (Grand Rapids, MI: Zondervan, 1992), 61-82.

5. Eric J. Sundquist, *King's Dream* (New Haven, CT: Yale University Press, 2009), 100.

6. Rosemarie Jarski, *Words from the Wise* (New York: Skyhorse Publishing, 2007), 199.

10. Saturday: I'm So Excited About Heaven

1. C.S. Lewis, *Mere Christianity* (New York: Macmillan, 1960), 119.

2. I encourage you to read and meditate on the complete lyrics of Wesley's hymn, which you can find at www.hymnary.org/text/christ_the_lord_is_risen_today_wesley.

3. The King James Version fetchingly called these heavenly homes "mansions." I have heard some deride this translation, pointing out that the Greek word merely means "dwelling places" or "residences" rather than palatial manors. I consider such criticisms to be shortsighted. After all, a heavenly home is, by definition, in heaven. Some people think it will be an existence in an entirely new dimension, higher than our current four-dimensional reality. But whatever the case dimensionally, heaven surely is a vast improvement over earth, exponentially better in every regard. The smallest shack in heaven would be a better place to live than any palace on earth. Thus, from our earthbound perspective, I find "mansions" to be a perfectly appropriate word, much better than the pedestrian "rooms" or prosaic "dwelling places."

4. Randy Alcorn, *The Treasure Principle* (Colorado Springs, CO: Multnomah Books, 2001), 50.

5. For further study about heaven, I suggest these books as two good places to begin: Randy Alcorn, *Heaven* (Carol Stream, IL: Tyndale House Publishers, 2004) and Joni Eareckson Tada, *Heaven* (Grand Rapids, MI: Zondervan, 1995).

Acknowledgments

Paul thanked the Christians in Philippi, "Even when I was in Thessalonica you sent help more than once" (Philippians 4:16 NLT). In a similar vein, I would like to say to my dear family, friends, and church members, "Even when I was on sabbatical, writing this book, you sent help more than once." Specifically,

- Thanks to my wife, Amy, the love of my life and the one who has taught me most about promise-making and promise-keeping. Thanks also to our three children, Micah, Noah, and Jesse, who are the brightest joys in our lives.

- Thanks to my parents, Don and Gay Stedman, whose almost seventy years of marriage is a monumental example of the blessing of promises, and to my siblings Randy and Teri, both of whom I treasure deeply.

- Thanks also to my in-laws, Dean and Marcia Holst, whose familial and faith promises helped shape and form my wife into the woman she is, and who have always been so gracious and loving to me. It is to Dean and Marcia that I have respectfully dedicated this book.

- Thanks to my edit team members, who once again tremendously helped me wordsmith each page and correct my many mistakes. Thanks especially to Nicholas Domich, Carol Peterson, Bev Graham, Vivian Jones, and Lori Clark. I appreciate your efforts and insights more than I can possibly express. A thousand times, thank you.

- A double thanks is due to Lori Clark, my assistant for over seventeen years. Her faithful, loyal, and excellent service has helped me immeasurably.

- Thanks also to my literary agent, Janet Grant, and to the team at Harvest House, including Terry Glaspey and

Rod Morris. For years I have dreamed of helping Christians improve their prayer lives and assisting pastors to better train their congregations in prayer. Thank you so much Janet, Terry, and Rod for your partnership in turning my longings into reality.

- Thanks also to our dear church, Adventure Christian Church of Roseville, California, for your love and support over the twenty-one years I was blessed to serve as senior pastor. Serving God in this church was—and still is—a blessing beyond what I had ever dreamed possible. Thanks also to the staff, led by Gil Stieglitz, for your unceasing friendship and support.

- Speaking of our church, as this book was unfolding, God also turned the pages of our lives and opened a fantastic new chapter. I deeply felt, by the urging of the Spirit, that it was time for me to hand the baton of senior pastor to a new leader, one who could open a new and catalytic chapter in our church's life. Thank you to all the elders and church members who had the courage and vision to embrace this change. Thanks also to Tommy Politz, who is the new senior pastor of our church (now renamed Hillside Christian Church). I am humbled and honored to still call this my home church and the base from which I can minister.

- Above all I want to thank our Lord and Savior Jesus Christ, who gave us, undeserving as we were, his "great and precious promises." He is the ultimate example of promise-making and promise-keeping, for he is "Faithful and True" and "no matter how many promises God has made, they are 'Yes' in Christ."

About the Author

Dr. Rick Stedman is a collector of classic rock-and-roll vinyl LPs, bookaholic, author, philosopher, pastor, and devoted husband and father. For two decades he founded and led Adventure Christian Church (now renamed Hillside Christian Church) in Roseville, California, a church that in ten years grew from zero to five thousand in spite of the fact that Rick listens to his records as he writes his sermons.

Rick has graduate degrees in theology, philosophy, and ministry, and has been a guest on various radio shows, including *Focus on the Family*. For relaxation he likes to read, ride on his tractor, tinker in his workshop, and watch movies with his wife and best friend, Amy.

Further resources for praying the promises of Jesus, including a printable *Praying the Promises of Jesus* bookmark, small group study guides, sermon outlines, illustrations, and other pastoral resources, are available at rickstedman.com. Rick can be reached at rick@rickstedman.com, and his blog is also available at rickstedman.com.

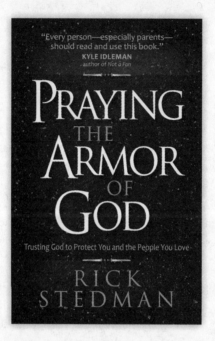

Praying the Armor of God

The Bible is clear: This world is a spiritual battle zone that every day puts us and those we love in harm's way from enemy attacks. Satan is relentless, and human defenses are no match for his dark devices. What can you do to protect yourself and your family?

Pastor Rick Stedman proposes the solution: You need to put on the armor of God through prayer. As you follow his easy-to-remember method, you will learn to

- focus on a specific piece of armor for each day of the week
- spend quality time with God as you pray biblically and effectively
- become empowered to face each day's battles and to protect those you love

Praise for Praying the Armor of God

"This is a great way to protect those you love spiritually. Every person—especially parents—should read and use this book."—Kyle Idleman, Southeast Christian Church, Louisville, Kentucky

"In this fantastic book, Rick Stedman models for us how to pray for those we love. *Praying the Armor of God* teaches us a lot about the heart of God and the joy of taking our cares and concerns to him. This is a book to read, apply, and share with others."—Jud Wilhite, Central Christian Church, Las Vegas, Nevada

"Praying on the armor of God has never been so practical. Rick Stedman has provided for us a simple way to bring God's protective power into the lives of the people we love."—David Butts, chairman, America's National Prayer Committee

"The hardest thing about the Christian life is that it is so *daily*. As a seasoned pastor, faithful disciple, and outstanding communicator, Rick Stedman has written this practical and relevant guide for daily victory. Christ's sufficient provision of spiritual armor is available to every believer. This book makes it readily applicable to your heart and your home, seven days a week."—Daniel Henderson, president, Strategic Renewal